SOUTH YORKSHIRE YESTERDAY

South Yorkshire Yesterday

Glimpses of the Past

Melvyn Jones

Smith Settle

First published in 2003 by
Smith Settle
an imprint of Dalesman Publishing Company Ltd
Stable Courtyard
Broughton Hall
Skipton
North Yorkshire
BD23 3AZ
www.dalesman.co.uk

ISBN 1 85825 187 7

Set in Monotype Bembo

Designed, printed and bound by
SMITH SETTLE PRINTING & BOOKBINDING LTD
Ilkley Road, Otley, West Yorkshire LS21 3JP

Contents

Acknowledgements

I would like to acknowledge the help of the following in providing information and illustrations, and granting permission to quote from copyright material:

Colin Howes, environmental records officer at Doncaster Museum, for making available to me a copy of his study of hedgerows and landscape in the parish of Fishlake for 'A Unique Historical Rural Landscape' on pages 49-55.

Milton (Peterborough) Estates Company and the Head of Leisure Services, Sheffield City Council, for permission to quote from the Wentworth Woodhouse Muniments in 'Leasing, Building and Baptising' on pages 67-79 and in 'Whit Walks and Going a-Maying' on pages 153-162.

Mrs C J Durdy of Tickhill for permission to quote from William Nesbitt's diaries which are in her personal possession in 'Blacklegs, Bludgeons and Broken Heads' on pages 88-95.

Captain Alex and Mrs Joan Swann for providing the painting of Alfred and Margaret Gatty (the chess players) on page 97 and the photograph of Alfred Scott-Gatty on page 100; Nicholas Baldwin, archivist, Great Ormond Street Hospital, London for the *Aunt Judy's Magazine* cot photograph on page 98; and the Head of Leisure Services, Sheffield City Council, for permission to reproduce on page 101 the watercolour of 'Julie and Dot — The Harvest Field 1865' by Margaret Scott Gatty which is part of a collection of watercolours and pen and pencil sketches (MD 2688, fol 27) in Sheffield Archives, presented to the archives by Colonel William Mackenzie Smith of Barnes Hall, son of Margaret Scott Gatty.

The librarian, Windsor Castle, for permission to quote from Queen Victoria's Journal in 'When the Wild Beast Show Came to Town' on page 108; and John and Ann Hartley who kindly lent me a copy of *Bostock & Wombwells No 1 Royal Menagerie catalogue* (1919).

Mrs Joan Swann, David Smith's daughter, for permission to use any material from his *Blackwoods Magazine* 'A Yorkshire Christmas' article in 'Christmas at the Squire's House' on pages 115-122.

Helen Larae Free Vanderbeek Kerr for permission to tell the story of the emigration of George Wadsworth from her book *George Allen Wadsworth — Pilley to Panaca* (Gateway Press, Baltimore, 1983) and to use the photograph of George Allen Wadworth on page ii of that book in 'From Tankersley to Nevada' on pages 123-132.

Mrs Marjorie Copley, the daughter of Arthur Andrews, for generously allowing me to quote at length from her father's manuscript account of his childhood in 'Making Ends Meet' on pages 133-142.

I should particularly like to thank BBC Radio Sheffield personnel for their support, especially David Markwell and Jamie Campbell; Eric Leslie for his watercolours and drawings; Bob Warburton for the maps; Neil Donovan for help with disks; and last but not least, my wife Joan for proofreading, her many helpful suggestions, her photography and her forbearance.

Illustrative Acknowledgements

Pauline & Michael Bentley, pp77, 78; Chapeltown and High Green Archive, pp89, 92, 95, 117, 119, 122, 124, 140, 142, 155, 156; Marjorie Copley, p134; Crown Copyright reserved, p150; William Dunigan, pp72, 76, 79; Stanley Ellam, p157; Julie Goddard, p138; Great Ormond Street Hospital, p98; John Gregory, p137; Laura Hicks, p159; Joan Jones, pp29, 37, 38, 39, 42, 46, 55, 57, 59, 60, 61, 62, 63, 64, 66; Helen Larae Free Vanderbeek Kerr, p130; Eric Leslie, pp69, 113, 121, 136, 161; Commander Michael Saunders-Watson of Rockingham Castle, p75; Chris Sharp, p143; Head of Leisure Services, Sheffield City Council, p101; Joyce Smith, p116; Captain Alex and Mrs Joan Swann, pp97, 100; Joan Swann, p120; Bob Warburton, p18; Mick Womersley, p141.

Foreword

by Tony Capstick

Melvyn Jones was a regular and very valued contributor to my afternoon show on BBC Radio Sheffield from January 1998 to March 2002. His knowledge of the history of our area is superb. He has led my listeners and me on a journey of discovery over the years. We have learned about the characters, the villains, the aristocracy (sometimes all at once), the origins of the place-names where we live, industry and the impact it has had on the environment, and much more. And he has done it with skill and flair and above all an enthusiasm that is enthralling. This book is based on the things he has taught us, and if you didn't hear them the first time round on Wednesday afternoons, then you are in for a full treat. If you did hear them, then here is a second chance to savour them at your leisure — Mel's midweek magic.

The author (*left*) with Tony Capstick at BBC Radio Sheffield.

Introduction

When David Markwell, a producer at BBC Radio Sheffield, telephoned me in January 1998 and asked me if I'd like to be a regular contributor with a 'local history spot' on Tony Capstick's show, I hesitated. Could I talk about a subject for about twenty-five minutes each week? How many local history subjects were there to talk about? How enthusiastic would be the response from listeners? I took a deep breath and said yes. By March 2002 I had completed 150 programmes with host Tony Capstick, and since changes to the schedule in April the programmes continue on the Rony Robinson show.

It works like this. About Thursday or Friday I think of a topic for the following week's show and put together some notes. And these are posted to BBC Radio Sheffield over the weekend. Tony and Rony both have a genuine interest in history and considerable knowledge of the subject. Moreover, they always do their home-work, and ask pertinent questions and make perceptive comments whatever the subject. And the response from listeners has been marvellous, with phone calls during and letters following programmes, some of them with interesting material that has been incorporated into later programmes.

The eighteen chapters in the book represent both the worked-up contents of individual programmes and the distillation of groups of programmes on related subjects. They are also copiously illustrated with photographs, drawings, paintings and maps, something impossible to do on radio.

Melvyn Jones
Thorpe Hesley

Were Your Ancestors Vikings?

If you can trace your family back for several hundred years in South Yorkshire, there is a very good chance that your roots go back much further and that indeed you carry Viking genes. Only DNA fingerprinting would show this, but even without going as far as this, it can be shown that the influence of our Viking ancestors is all around us.

The former presence of the Vikings is still very marked in the South Yorkshire landscape through the wide distribution of Viking names of villages and hamlets, and in the distinctive street names of the largest towns. The Vikings also gave their names to ancient administrative systems in South Yorkshire. They also made a great contribution to our vocabulary — both words in standard English and in the South Yorkshire dialect. Lastly, many of us carry Viking surnames.

The word 'Viking' was the name given by the Anglo-Saxon population of England to the raiders from Scandinavia in the late eighth and ninth centuries. The name probably originated from 'Viken', the area around the Oslo fjord in Norway, but it soon came to be a synonym for a pirate or raider. The Vikings who came to Britain as traders, raiders and then settlers were from Norway and Denmark. The Norwegians eventually settled in the Shetland and Orkney Islands, the Hebrides, the west coast of Scotland, the Isle of Man, the east coast of Ireland and north-west England. They also sailed on westwards and established colonies in Iceland, Greenland and North America. The Danes eventually settled in eastern England from the Tweed to the Thames.

The Viking age is said to have begun in AD 793 when the monastery of Lindisfarne was raided and plundered. 'Never before has such terror appeared in Britain as we have now suffered from a pagan race', wrote Alcuin, a monk from York, who was at that time a teacher and advisor to Charlemagne at Aachen. The raiding continued in the first half of the ninth century, and then in AD 865 a great Danish army arrived under the leadership of Halfdan, who conquered the Anglo-Saxon kingdoms of Northumbria (which stretched from the Tweed to the Humber), the whole of East Anglia and the eastern half of the midland kingdom of Mercia. After gaining their military victories, the Danish war leaders were joined by agricultural settlers, although there is still debate about how large the agricultural settlement was. *The Anglo-Saxon Chronicle*, the annals of Anglo-Saxon history begun in the mid-ninth century, recorded that the Danes had permanently settled in Yorkshire by 875. Soon after 886 a treaty between the Danes and King Alfred, Saxon king of Wessex, formally recognised the area ruled by the Danes, called *Danelaw*, which included all the territory north and east of Watling Street (the modern A5) which ran from London to Chester. Within Danelaw the physical presence of the Danes, their institutions and language had great impact.

The question naturally arises: why did they settle in South Yorkshire? Basically they were short of land. Climatic improvement meant good harvests in their homelands which in turn led to population growth, which caused population pressure. They had also perfected the arts of boat-building and navigation at sea. They therefore had a reason for emigrating and a means of accomplishing it. The Danes must have come up the Humber and entered South Yorkshire through the lower reaches of the Don and Trent, and then up the valleys of the Dearne, Don and Rother. They re-named villages and farms, established new settlements, imposed their administrative systems and introduced many new words into the evolving language of the region's inhabitants.

Viking place-names

The most obvious legacy left to South Yorkshire by the Danish Vikings is the substantial number of place-names of Viking origin that pepper the landscape. These are made up of either Old Norse words, a combination of Old Norse and Old English (Anglo-Saxon) elements, or are 'Scandinavianised' versions of Old English names.

The most common Scandinavian place-name element in Yorkshire as a whole is -by. There are 210 -by place-names recorded in *Domesday Book* of 1086 in Yorkshire, with another sixty-nine first recorded in post-*Domesday* medieval records. When used by the Danes it meant town or village, and when used by the Norwegians it meant a farm. The modern 1:50,000 Ordnance Survey maps that cover South Yorkshire (sheets 110 and 111) record ten places containing this place-name element. All but one of these is in the eastern half of the county, five of them — Barnby Dun, Scawsby, Balby, Cadeby and Denaby — beside the River Don, a major colonisation route. With two

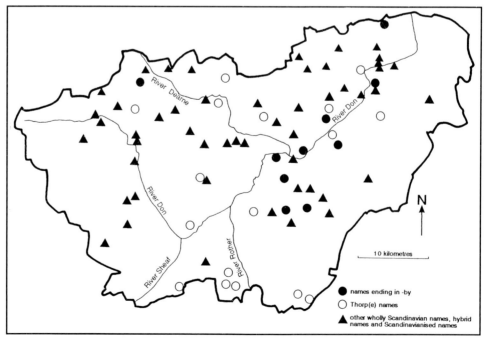

Distribution of Viking place-names in South Yorkshire.

Hesley Hall at Thorpe Hesley. Hesley Hall is in the ancient parish of Ecclesfield. Around the site of the hall, by the time of *Domesday*, a small village with the Danish Viking name of *Thorp* had been established.

exceptions these -*by* names are made up of the suffix -*by* and a prefix in the form of an Old Norse personal name, for example Kati's farm or village (Cadeby), Helgi's farm or village (Hellaby), and Malti's farm or village (Maltby). The two exceptions are Firsby and Denaby. Firsby means 'the farm or village of the Frisians' and Denaby means 'the farm or village of the Danes'.

The second most common Danish Viking place-name element found in South Yorkshire is -*thorp*. It occurs seventeen times on the 1:50,000 Ordnance Survey maps, and there is almost a dozen 'lost' settlements (ie settlements whose names appear in old documents but which do not exist anymore on the ground) that contained the -*thorp* element. It means, as it does in Denmark, an outlying farm or hamlet dependent on a larger, earlier settlement. In other parts of Danelaw there is sometimes a -*by* settlement with the same prefix as a neighbouring -*thorp* settlement, showing very directly the link between a pre-existing village and a dependent farm or hamlet, as in Barkby and Barkbythorpe in Leicestershire and Ashwell and Ashwellthorpe in Norfolk. The nearest equivalent of this in South Yorkshire is the village of Thorpe Hesley, which grew up mainly in Kimberworth and Wentworth townships beside the presumably pre-existing Anglo-Saxon settlement of Hesley just across the parish boundary in Ecclesfield. As with the -*by* settlements, the prefixes of a number of the -*thorp* settlements are personal names, for example Goldthorpe (Golda's outlying farm or outlet). Others mention an occupation as in Shipmanthorpe (shepherd's outlying farm or hamlet) or describe a site as in Wildthorpe, a settlement that appeared in *Domesday Book* but is now lost. Joseph Hunter in his *South Yorkshire* (1819) remarks that at the site of Wildthorpe on 'that high and exposed point between [High] Melton and Cadeby there is a tradition that a village once stood, and that it was blown away' — in a violent storm.

There are many other wholly Old Norse names, besides some of the *-by* and *-thorpe* names already mentioned. These include Thurnscoe (*thyrne skogr*, thorny wood), Guilthwaite (clearing (*thwaite*) in a ravine (*gil*)), Wath upon Dearne (*vath*, ford), Scholes (*skali*, sheds, temporary buildings), Storrs (*storth*, wood), and Staincross (*steinn cros*, stone cross,) of which more below.

Then there are also 'hybrid names', with one element Old English and the other Old Norse, showing the mixing of the Anglo-Saxon and Danish Viking populations and their languages. Among these are Thurlstone (the farmstead (Old English *tun*) belonging to *Thurulf* (Old Danish personal name)); Wickersley (Vikar's woodland clearing — *Vikar* is an Old Norse or Old Danish personal name and *leah* (woodland clearing) is Old English); Micklebring (large (Old Norse *micel*) slope (Old English *brink*); and Grenoside (quarried hillside: Old English *graefen* (excavation, quarry), Old Norse *haugr* (hill), and the Modern English 'side' (first recorded in the seventeenth century), giving Gren–o–side).

But perhaps the two most intriguing hybrid names belong to two places lying side by side beside the River Don: Conisbrough and Denaby. Conisbrough simply means the king's fortress, from the Old Norse *konungr* (king) and Old English *burh* meaning fortress or stronghold. The name appeared in *Domesday Book* as *Coningesborc, Coninges-burg* and *Cuningeburg*. The medieval chronicler Geoffrey of Monmouth in his *Historia Regum Britanniae* (*The History of the Kings of Britain*, c1136) called it '*oppidum Kaerconan quod nunc Cununsburg appellatur*', 'the king's town or city of Kaerconan that is now called Cunungsburg'; *Caer* in *Caerkonan* is the Celtic word for a fortified site, as in Caernarvon or Carlisle. Denaby means 'village of the Danes', but the first element is from the Old English *Denige* (of the Danes), so it must have been a name given to a Danish settlement by the surrounding Anglo-Saxon population.

Lastly there are Scandinavianised names where the Old Norse speakers substituted the Old Norse element for the Old English even when the original Old English sound could have been pronounced by Old Norse speakers, for example *steinn* for *stan* (stony) as in Stainforth, Stainton and Stainborough. However, there were some sounds in Old English that were unfamiliar to Old Norse speakers and they substituted sounds with which they were familiar. For example, they substituted *th* for *d* as in *breithe* for *brad* (broad), eg Braithwell; *rauthr* for *read* (red) as in Rawmarsh; and *methel* (which became *mel*) for *middel*, as in High Melton which was recorded as Middelton, Mideltone and Medeltone in *Domesday Book* but which had become written as Methelton by 1208 and Melton by 1248. In the same way they also probably substituted *sk* for *sh* as in Askern (corner where ash trees grew) and probably in Skelbrooke and Skellow, the first element in both of these names probably being the Scandinavianised *skel* for the Old English *scel* (hut or shieling, pronounced 'shel'). Finally they substituted *c* for *ch*, as in Carlton which would originally have been Charlton (homestead of the churls or freemen).

Conisbrough, looking along Church Street, towards the church which contains much work of the pre-*Domesday* period when the village also got its hybrid Old Norse and Old English name.

In addition to these village and town names, there are the names of fields, lanes and minor places that have survived that show the Old Norse language was once used throughout South Yorkshire to name a wide variety of rural and urban places. For example, three words indicating low-lying, damp or wet ground have survived throughout the area. These are *kjarr* (marsh), *holmr* (island in a marsh) and *eng* (water meadow). *Kjarr* survives in Deepcar and Elsecar in the west and central parts of South Yorkshire, and in many low-lying districts in the east including Huggin Carr south of Hatfield Woodhouse, Wrancarr east of Askern and Flashley Carr east of Moss. Likewise *holmr* survives in many field names as well as in the names of a number of minor settlements such as in Holmes in the Don Valley south of Rotherham, and in Almholme, Shaftholme and Lindholme in the eastern lowlands. Of Lindholme, Joseph Hunter writing in his *South Yorkshire* said it was 'a little island in Hatfield-turf-moor, [which] could be approached only in times of extreme drought or frost'. The use of *eng*, usually spelt as 'ing', was widespread in the west as well as the east for damp meadowland. Every village in the Dearne Valley had its ings, the most well known in recent years being Wath Ings, the wetland bird reserve. Further east, ings are widespread, and the 1:25,000 Ordnance Survey Explorer map (sheet 279) shows Great Ing, Town Ing and Low Ings in Fishlake parish alone.

Other minor Old Norse names include *bekkr* (stream) as in Firbeck and Howell Beck; *kirkja* (church) as in Kirkhouse Green , Kirk Bramwith and Kirk Sandall; and *hlathe* (barn) as in Laith Croft at Dodworth and Laithes Lane at Athersley in Barnsley. Although occurring in rural areas, the Old Norse word *gata*, now spelt 'gate', meaning

Castlegate street sign, Tickhill.

lane or street, is a Viking word most associated with urban areas. Barnsley has its Eastgate and Westgate, and Church Gate used to be Kirkgate; central Doncaster contains Baxter Gate (street of the bakers), High and Low Fisher Gate, French Gate, Friars Gate, Hallgate, St George Gate, and St Sepulchre Gate; Rotherham has Bridgegate, Doncaster Gate, Moorgate (the street leading to the moor or common) and Wellgate; Sheffield has Fargate; and Tickhill's main streets are Westgate, Castlegate and Northgate. The word was also introduced into the mining industry at an early date for the main underground roadway in a colliery (the main gate), a name that has remained in use to the present day.

Viking administrative divisions

The Vikings also gave their names to several old administrative divisions in South Yorkshire. South Yorkshire is, of course, part of the former West Riding, 'riding' being the Danish Viking name (*thrithungr*) for a third part. At a more local level, counties were divided into smaller units for judicial and administrative matters. Outside Danelaw, groups of parishes were known as *hundreds*, but inside Danelaw they were known as *wapentakes*. It is believed that wapentake denoted a meeting at which agreement was shown by brandishing weapons. South Yorkshire was divided into three wapentakes — Lower Strafforth, Upper Strafforth and Staincross. Strafforth wapentake (recorded in *Domesday Book* as '*Strafordes wapentac*') is presumed to take its name from a meeting place at Strafford Sands in Mexborough where there was a major crossing of the River Don. The Staincross wapentake is named after its meeting place, the former hamlet of Staincross 2½ miles (4km), north-west of Barnsley, where presumably a stone cross stood.

A common Viking practice was the holding of open-air assemblies called *things*. Each district held an *allthing* where new local laws were agreed, and court proceedings took place. The Isle of Man still has its *Tynwald* (*thing* (assembly), *-vollr* (field)), the annual assembly proclaiming newly enacted laws. It is generally believed that the names of a group of settlements to the south-east of Rotherham — Morthen, Brampton en le Morthen and Laughton in le Morthen — signify the former existence of such an assembly that was held on a common (moor) in the district and was called the *moor-thing*. Significantly a document of 1345 recorded a meadow between Upper Whiston and Morthen called *Tourneberg*. The word *Tourneberg* means hill (*berg*) where a court (*tourn*) was held.

At a more local level still, the Viking word *bierlow* (Old Norse *byar-log*) was in the past attached to the names of Brampton, Brightside, Ecclesall, Greasbrough and the four sub-divisions of the large township of Bradfield (Bradfield, Dungworth, Walder-shelf and Westnall). The name Brampton Bierlow still appears as the name of the civil parish on the 1:25,000 Ordnance Survey Explorer map sheet 278. Bierlow means 'the law of the village', and when attached to the name of a village simply meant a small district in which local laws had been enacted to deal with minor disputes. The term is still used generally today for local laws or 'by-laws'.

Viking language

One of the most important aspects of the Viking heritage is the part that these peoples had in simplifying the English language and bringing into it a greater variety of vocabulary. Before the arrival of the Danes, Old English was an inflected language, ie it relied on words having different word-endings to convey their precise meaning. But interaction between the Danes, who did not understand these inflections, and the Saxons, led to their virtual extinction. At the same time the Saxons and their descendants — who of course inter-married with the Danes — incorporated as many as a thousand Old Norse words into the English language. These include such commonly used words such as drown, crawl, get, hit, leg, scare, skull, skin, and skirt.

The Danish settlers also supplied a substantial number of words that have not entered the standard English language, but persist in the Yorkshire dialect. A few of those still used in South Yorkshire include *addle* (to earn), *band* (string), *dee* (to die), *flit* (to move away), *gawp* (to stare), *laik* (to play), *lig* (to lie)), *lug* (ear), *skitters* (diarrhoea), *skrike* (to shriek) and *teem* (to pour).

Viking surnames

Lastly, many of us carry Old Norse surnames. These come in four different forms: those named after a place with an Old Norse name; those in the form of an Old Norse personal name; those from an Old Norse nickname; and those from an occupation. Those surnames derived from a place with an Old Norse place-name are the most common, indicating that the person who was given that name was a migrant from that place at the time in the Middle Ages when hereditary names were being fixed. Among names in this category found in local telephone directories include *Askwith* or *Asquith* (Askwith is a place in West Yorkshire meaning ash wood); *Micklethwaite* (another place in West Yorkshire meaning 'big clearing in a wood'); *Maltby* (the South Yorkshire

The village children of Scholes in 1906. The name Scholes, which is also a common surname, means sheds or temporary dwellings in Old Norse.

village whose name in Old Norse means 'Malti's village'); *Scholes* (the name of one village in South Yorkshire and two in West Yorkshire meaning 'sheds' or 'temporary buildings'); and *Thorpe* (which could be from any one of the more than 200 places in England called Thorpe). Names from Old Norse personal names include *Grime* or *Grimes* (Grimr), *Swain* (Sveinn) and *Knott* (Canute, which is also a nickname meaning 'thickset'). Surnames derived from nicknames include *Tait* or *Tate* (cheerful) and *Crook(e)* (crooked or hunchback); occupational names include *Thacker* (thatcher) and *Skinner*.

Ivanhoe, Robin Hood and all That
Myth and Legend in Medieval Times

Two of the greatest legendary figures of medieval England have a strong South Yorkshire connection. One, Robin Hood, was already a popular mythical figure before the end of the Middle Ages; the other, Ivanhoe, was a nineteenth-century literary creation, but the regional setting of the book *Ivanhoe*, partly fictionalised and partly real, is in South Yorkshire.

In connection with the book *Ivanhoe*, it is worth considering first its author, Sir Walter Scott (1771–1832). He was trained as a lawyer, and in 1799 became deputy sheriff of Selkirk and in 1806 clerk of session of Edinburgh. He took a great interest in the folklore and history of the Scottish borders, and in 1802–3 published the region's traditional songs and ballads under the title *Minstrelsy of the Scottish Border*. In that book he included some of his own work in imitation of the traditional ballads he had collected. He then published a whole series of his long poems over the next decade or so. Such was his celebrity that he was offered the poet laureateship, but declined it.

He then gave up poetry in favour of prose and became the first writer of historical novels, composed at the beginning and end of his working day. These appeared anonymously as he believed novel writing was below the dignity of an eminent lawyer and country gentleman. This anonymity was kept for a decade. His novels include *Waverley*, *The Bride of Lammermoor* (which he wrote in a fortnight), *The Heart of Midlothian*, *Quentin Durward*, *Guy Mannering*, *Rob Roy*, and the most famous, *Ivanhoe* (1819). He was made a baronet in 1820. By that time he had become the most famous Scotsman alive and his home at Abbotsford attracted distinguished visitors from all over Europe. He was the model for Alexandre Dumas and Victor Hugo, the French writers of historical fiction.

However, in 1826 disaster struck. The publishing house of Ballantyne in which he was a partner collapsed with debts of £250,000. He then devoted the rest of his life to repaying the debt: 'this right hand shall work it off', he declared. The debt was fully paid after his death from the sale of his copyrights. In the pantheon of great storytellers, critics place him beside Homer and Shakespeare.

The novel *Ivanhoe* came to be written because he thought his readers would tire of Scottish-based historical romances. Basically *Ivanhoe* is a 'ripping yarn' about right overcoming wrong and true love conquering all, with large doses of medieval chivalry and armed combat, all in ravishing settings mostly in the wild country of — wait for it — Rotherham Metropolitan Borough. It has been dramatised, made into an opera by Rossini, and adapted for film and television.

It is set in the late twelfth century and contains a substantial number of main characters. First there are the brave and honest but oppressed Saxons represented by the eponymous hero, Sir Wilfred of Ivanhoe; his father, Cedric of Rotherwood; and the love of his life, the beautiful Lady Rowena. Then there are the dastardly Normans represented by Prince John, Sir Brian de Bois Guilbert, Sir Reginald Front de Boeuf, Philip de Malvoisin (the royal forest head ranger, whose name means 'bad neighbour') and Prior Aymer. Also playing important roles are the Jew, Isaac of York, and his beautiful daughter Rebecca. Isaac is despised by the Normans for being a non-believer, moneylender and pawnbroker, and his daughter is lusted after by Sir Brian de Bois-Guilbert. Then there is King Richard the Lion Heart who has just arrived in England from captivity in Austria. (Richard reigned from 1189–99.) And last but not least, there are Robin Hood, Friar Tuck and the outlaws of Sherwood Forest.

The added bonus of *Ivanhoe* for potential readers in South Yorkshire is that the medieval landscape is supposed to be the local one. Sheffield, Rotherham, Doncaster, Wharncliffe and Wentworth all get honourable mentions. And all these places are apparently small islands of settlement in a sea of primaeval forest. As Sir Walter puts it in his opening sentence:

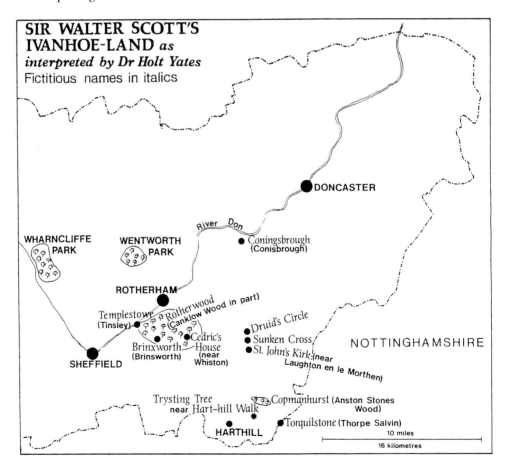

Dr Holt Yates's interpretation of Scott's fictional geography of South Yorkshire.

'In that pleasant district of merry England which is watered by the River Don, there extended in ancient times a large forest, covering the greater part of the beautiful hills and valleys which lie between Sheffield and the pleasant town of Doncaster.'

Scott also invented a whole set of fictitious local places, for example, Rotherwood, Templestowe, Copmanhurst and Torquilstone — reckoned by Victorian antiquary, Dr Holt Yates of Wickersley, to be Whiston, Tinsley, Anston Stones Wood and Thorpe Salvin respectively.

Historical inaccuracy as well as straightforward fictionalisation is everywhere. There is a general belief — fed by Scott and other writers of historical romance — that, in the Middle Ages, England was covered in woodland. As someone who has just re-read *Ivanhoe* said to me: 'Scott makes it sound ever so leafy'. The truth of the matter could not be more different. Only fifteen per cent of South Yorkshire was wooded at *Domesday*, a century before the period in which *Ivanhoe* was set. The comparable figure for Nottinghamshire is twelve per cent, and for Leicestershire — where Ashby, the scene of a tournament, one of the important set-pieces in the book takes place — a staggeringly low three per cent. And of course woodland clearance went on apace after 1086. Moreover, much of the woodland at *Domesday* in the East and North Midlands in the eleventh and twelfth centuries was wood pasture in which trees were often widely spaced and which also contained large areas of heathland, and cultivation and settlement — like the New Forest today. The boundless stretches of 'wildwood' suggested by Sir Walter Scott had long since disappeared.

But what about Sherwood Forest, which plays such a central role in the book, I hear my critics cry. Interestingly, Scott often uses the terms forest and woodland interchangeably, and the term forest had another, purely legal meaning in the Middle Ages which had nothing to do with trees. It referred to land under forest law where only the king could hunt deer (and that of course is where Robin Hood comes in). Many royal forests had few trees. The Peak Forest, the royal forest in the Peak District of Derbyshire, for example, was mainly moorland.

There are other instances where Sir Walter paid scant regard to the facts. He had Conisbrough Castle ('Coningsburgh Castle') as the seat of a Saxon nobleman, whereas from the late elevnth century until the fourteenth century it was the seat of Norman lords, the de Warennes.

He also invented a succession of roles for Robin Hood and his Merry Men, including Friar Tuck. Scott says in the book's opening paragraph: 'Here also flourished in ancient times those bands of gallant outlaws whose deeds have been rendered so popular in English song'. This is an opportune point to turn our attention to the mythical figure of Robin Hood and his followers. Was he a real person? If not, who created the legend and why? Would he or his legend have existed in the late twelfth century when *Ivanhoe* was set? Was the Robin Hood of legend said to have operated in the area in which Scott set *Ivanhoe*? And did he rob the rich and give to the poor?

The first written reference to the legend of Robin Hood was in about 1377 when a character in William Langland's *Piers Plowman* says he knows of rhymes of Robin Hood. The earliest surviving written evidence of the legend itself is derived from surviving ballads and a play. The first is a manuscript called *Robin Hood and the Monk*

Conisbrough Castle, portrayed by Scott as the home of the Saxon nobleman Athelstane. It is said that Scott first saw Conisbrough Castle when he was being carried south by coach from Scotland to visit the battleground of Waterloo.

and dates to about 1450. Another is a manuscript called *Robin Hood and the Potter* which dates from 1503. A fragment of a manuscript dated about 1475 mentions Friar Tuck as a member of Robin Hood's band. By the beginning of the sixteenth century the legend was attracting the attention of printers, and a number of printed versions of what is called the *A Lyttell Gest of Robyn Hode* and which appeared in a number of different versions from c1495–c1530. The *Gest* is a long poem. At the beginning the scene is the outlaws' camp at a place called Barnsdale, and the company includes Little John, Much the Miller's son and Will Scarlock (ie Scarlett).

The medieval legend contains many items which have passed down to the present day: the locale in Sherwood Forest and on the Great North Road at Barnsdale on the South Yorkshire/West Yorkshire boundary; taking deer illegally in the king's forest; contests with the Sheriff of Nottingham (who is captured and slain); Robin Hood's prowess as an archer; and his fellow outlaws Little John, Much the Miller's son and Will Scarlett.

But the medieval legend does not refer to Robin Hood shooting an arrow to mark his grave; there is no Maid Marian; Robin Hood and Little John fighting with staves does not occur till the eighteenth century; the medieval legend only refers to 'Edward our comely king'; and there is no mention of Richard the Lion Heart. Neither is there any suggestion in the medieval ballads of overtaxing of the people or local or national oppression of the population (unless they are criminals) as the basis of Robin Hood's actions. The medieval Robin Hood was not a peasant and not a dispossessed

Robin Hood attacking the forest rangers of Sherwood.
From a woodcut by Thomas Bewick (1753–1828).

nobleman; he was a yeoman. He was not a rebel opposing the rich landowners nor a Saxon fighting Normans — as he is portrayed in *Ivanhoe*. Finally, there is little or nothing in the medieval legend about robbing the rich and giving to the poor.

The next question that must be addressed is: was Robin Hood a real person? It is highly likely that there was an original Robin Hood and, as we shall see, he must have lived no later than the first half of the thirteenth century. There were a number of possible candidates for the original Robin Hood, including two Robert Hoods in the manor of Wakefield.   In the Yorkshire Pipe Roll of 1230 there is a mention of a 'Robertus Hood fugitivus'. Whoever he was, he may have become a legend in his own lifetime. By the middle of the thirteenth century, eight people in south-east England were calling themselves or were being called by others 'Robinhood' as a nickname-surname. This suggests that the Robin Hood legend by that time was a national one. What is even more interesting is that five of the eight were suspected or known criminals. The earliest, so named in 1262, the leader of an outlaw gang, was called in one document Robert le Fevere (fevre = smith) and in a later one Robinhood. The name 'Robinhood' appears to have been becoming the surname of every suspected or known outlaw.

The surviving medieval ballads make it clear that the growing and fast-spreading legend was spoken, probably by wandering minstrels in the first place. Retainers in the houses where the minstrels declaimed their ballads (dramatic recitations rather than songs) probably spread the tales in the surrounding villages and towns. During the fifteenth century the Robin Hood legend became part of the May festival. Plays were based on the legend, and the friar and the Queen of the May, traditional characters in the morris dance, became Friar Tuck and Maid Marian. Robin Hood was the May queen's king. Robin Hood then became the centre of activities on May Day involving collecting money for the upkeep of the church — and this may be the origin of the robbing the rich to give to the poor part of the legend.

In the seventeenth century the various Robin Hood stories were embroidered, added to and changed (eg he became a nobleman, and was called Robin of Locksley). A Robert of Locksley (or Loxley) is said to have killed his father in an argument and fled to the woods to avoid arrest for murder. The stories were printed in chapbooks and broadsheets, and in the eighteenth century they were sung and more plays on the subject were written. By that time Robin Hood was part of an incipient heritage industry. A house in the Loxley Valley west of Sheffield was pointed out to visitors as his birthplace and the well at Barnsdale supported two inns. But the main tourism beneficiary was to become Nottingham and Sherwood. Sherwood Forest has a Robin Hood's larder, two caves, a stable, a well, and a grave — all of nineteenth-century origin. Sherwood is now the centre of 'Robin Hood's County' and the heritage centre there attracts visitors from far and wide. By the twentieth century Robin Hood was a well-known international figure. This was mainly the result of Hollywood, who got into the act early on — the first Robin Hood film was made in 1922 and starred Douglas Fairbanks. The most highly rated is the 1938 version, *The Adventures of Robin Hood*. It stars Errol Flynn as Sir Robin of Locksley, Basil Rathbone as Sir Guy of Gisbourne and Claud Rains as Prince John. Olivia de Havilland played Maid Marian. It was shot in the sun-filled forests of California, of course.

The medieval legend is set in two real locations much nearer home: Barnsdale and Sherwood. Barnsdale is on the Great North Road between Doncaster and Went-bridge on the boundary of West and South Yorkshire. This was where Robin Hood and the outlaws are said to have intercepted travellers on their way south. The medieval ballads mention a place called Sayles, and there is still a Sayles Plantation at Barnsdale, overlooking the Great North Road. Barnsdale is only twelve miles (19km) east of the manor of Wakefield with its thirteenth-century Robert or Robin Hoods, and only twenty miles (32km) east of Kirklees where legend has it that Robin Hood died. There is a Robin Hoods Well a mile (1.5km) or so south of Barnsdale Bar which was first recorded in 1622.

Sherwood Forest is the other main location. But everything about it is vague. Apart from Sherwood Forest itself, the town of Nottingham, with its castle, sheriff and St Mary's Church, no local detail is provided in early written sources — no named routes and no minor place names. This is in marked contrast to the Barnsdale area.

The many other 'Robin Hood' names are more likely to do with the spread of the legend rather than the spread of the activities of Robin Hood(s), for example: Robin Hoods Hill in Stanley near Wakefield; Robin Hoods Bower in the Loxley Valley (recorded in 1637); Robin Hoods Well in Hall Wood between Grenoside and High Green in Sheffield; Robin Hoods Stone near Whitby, and Robin Hoods Bay (both recorded by 1540). Little Johns Grave at Hathersage in north Derbyshire was known as early as the mid-sixteenth century.

Does all this debate about looking for reality in *Ivanhoe* and seeking definitive answers to questions about the Robin Hood legend really matter? Well, yes and no. If a reader is looking for the real medieval South Yorkshire — people and places — he or she should not seek the truth in *Ivanhoe*. It is a fabrication like a great deal of the

Robin Hoods Well on the Great North Road (A1) as illustrated in Joseph Hunter's *South Yorkshire* volume 2 (1831). It was designed by the architect Sir John Vanbrugh (1664–1726) for the earl of Carlisle. It lies less than two miles (3km) from Barnsdale Bar. Hunter gave the first known record of Robin Hood's well at Barnsdale as occurring at the beginning of the reign of Henry VII (1485–1509). Hunter was of the opinion that it got its name not because early ballads indicated that it was an area in which some of Robin Hood's adventures took place but because it was the location of medieval May Day celebrations with drama and dancing that included the characters of Robin Hood, Maid Marian and Friar Tuck.

modern heritage industry. But what a fabrication. Scott's triumph was to create a locale, a convincing set of heroes and villains, a fast-moving plot and a style of language that transcended issues such as factual accuracy. And that is to be expected of a man who, before turning his attention to South Yorkshire, had re-invented Scottish history and national identity — kilts, tartans, heather, bagpipes and all. *Ivanhoe* should be enjoyed for what it is — but where it purports to touch reality, it should be taken with a pinch of salt.

As for Robin Hood, it is probable that the Robin Hood legend did not emerge until after the period in which *Ivanhoe* was set by Scott, and it is clear that his role as folk hero, defender of the poor and oppressed against the rich and powerful, was one that developed centuries after the legend first emerged. What is equally clear is that the sphere of operations of this legendary figure, as documented in early written sources, did cover the parts of South Yorkshire in which much of *Ivanhoe* was set. As to whether Robin Hood belongs only to mythology and romance and not to history, and whether he should be considered to be a man of Nottinghamshire or a West or South York-shireman, I shall let readers draw their own conclusions from the evidence presented

'Buildid of Wodde'

The Lost Tradition of Timber-Framed Buildings

So naturally do the traditional stone buildings of South Yorkshire sit in the landscape that it is difficult to imagine that, except for religious and military structures, building in stone is largely a post-medieval characteristic. The walls, roofs, door jambs and window sills of ancient parish churches, country seats of the aristocracy and the gentry, old farmhouses and cottages, ruined castles and the remains of abbeys and priories appear, with a few exceptions, to be constructed almost entirely of local gritstone, sandstone or limestone. What is forgotten is that the stone keeps and curtain walls of the castles at Conisbrough and Tickhill were replacements for wooden structures, and that the stone walls of many medieval churches and surviving secular medieval buildings replaced or still encase a timber frame. Moreover, in old stone or brick buildings, the sandstone roofslabs or pantiles often rest on a substantial framework of locally grown timber.

As late as 1540 John Leland, the antiquary, on his six-year tour of England, described the town of Doncaster as 'buildid of woode, and the houses be slatid: yet is there great plenty of stone there about'. Later that century, in 1575–6, there is a detailed set of accounts relating to the building of a new house in Sheffield for William Dickenson, the agent for the earl of Shrewsbury's large Sheffield estate. The accounts give details of sixteen trees that were purchased, and payments that were made for 'posting' the timber (ie squaring and preparing joints in the main timber components), leading it from the wood to the house site, 'rearing' the house (ie lifting and securing the timber framework into position), and even 'Dawbinge' (ie covering the panels between the vertical posts or studs which was filled by wattle or stone slates with a mixture of clay and hay).

In fact it was not until the seventeenth century in South Yorkshire that stone and brick supplanted timber as the main building material, and there are records of about 300 buildings of timber-frame construction which still stand or are known to have been demolished since 1900, and there are others built of stone or brick but with medieval timber roof trusses.

It is in the surviving timber-framed buildings that trees from the region's medieval and Tudor woods can be seen. I say trees because the house carpenter (often called a housewright in old documents) did not obtain his timber in the form of ready sawn and shaped planks and beams — he selected trees in woods and hedges that would roughly square up to the dimensions of the components required with the minimum of shaping. For great beams a large tree with a diameter of fifteen to eighteen inches

Eleventh-century woodmen, carpenters and shipwrights as portrayed in the *Bayeux Tapestry*.

(38-46cm) would be chosen, and for rafters much younger trees about eight inches (20cm) in diameter would be felled.

The timber used was almost always oak, and it was sawn or shaped with an axe or adze while it was still 'green', for ease of working, as shown in the celebrated scenes from the Bayeux Tapestry, and carpentry techniques were developed to capitalise on the natural shapes and properties of the trees.

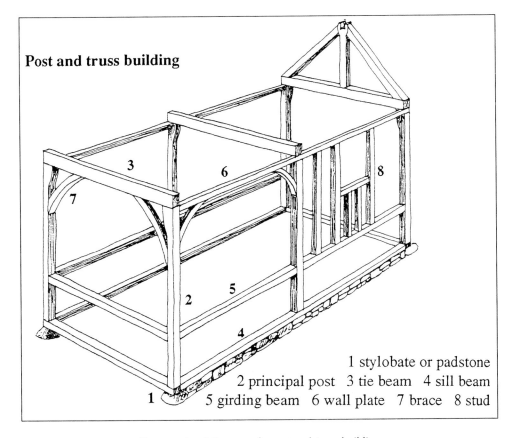

Post and truss building

1 stylobate or padstone
2 principal post   3 tie beam   4 sill beam
5 girding beam   6 wall plate   7 brace   8 stud

Constructional features of a post-and-truss building.

Interior of Whiston manorial barn, Rotherham.

There were two complementary traditions of timber-framed building in South Yorkshire: post-and-truss structures and cruck buildings. A post-and-truss building consisted of a series of trusses or cross frames formed by a pair of vertical posts (principal posts) standing on large stones (stylobates) and connected by tie beams. Longitudinally, the tops of the principal posts were connected by horizontal timbers, called wall plates (connecting the tops of the posts), girding beams (at mid-wall level) and sill beams (at or near ground level). In some cases the lower walls up to the girding beams were of stone. For extra stability, curved timber braces were used between principal post and wall plate, principal post and girding beam, and between principal post and tie beam. The walls, where not of stone, were framed by vertical timbers called studs, with the spaces between filled with wattle and daub, stone slates covered with plaster or horizontal split oak laths, again covered by plaster. The roofs were of the common rafter type or the principal rafter type. The rafters in common rafter roofs were strengthened by collars just below the apex; in principal rafter roofs in South Yorkshire, the principal rafters were supported by a vertical post rising from the tie beam, called a king-post. Surviving post-and-truss buildings of medieval or immediate post-medieval age include the thirteenth-century Whiston Manorial Barn, Nether Fold Farmhouse at Scholes, the Old Queens Head, Sheffield (timbers felled c1506–1510), Bishops' House, Sheffield (c1525) and the magnificent Gunthwaite Hall Barn (sixteenth century).

Whiston Manorial Barn is probably of thirteenth-century date. It originally consisted of five bays (a bay is the space between two trusses), but in the seventeenth century the building was extended by two more bays, extra principal posts were added and the original timber walls were replaced by stone. Whiston Manorial Barn is an example of an aisled post-and-truss building. In this type of structure, extra building width was achieved by erecting the long walls beyond the principal posts, to which they were connected by extensions to the roof trusses. Aisle ties (short sections of timber connecting the principal posts with the tops of the long walls) and wind braces (curved pieces of timber connecting the principal posts to the long walls) were added to strengthen the overall structure.

Bishops' House, an L-shaped yeoman's house built c1500–50, and now one of Sheffield's museums, was originally largely framed in timber, with a northern extension to the west wing being built in stone in the mid-seventeenth century. The original timber-framed house had two wings, the east wing containing the hall and the kitchen, and the west wing with a parlour and buttery on the ground floor and two chambers above on the first floor. Both wings have a post-and-truss structure in which the king-post roof is supported on a frame of vertical and horizontal oak timbers tied together with mortise and tenon joints and treenails (long wooden pegs). The timber framing may have continued almost to the ground, but there is a difference of opinion on this. At ground-floor level, except for the principal (corner)

Bishops' House, Sheffield, in 1823 as drawn by Edward Blore. The east wing is on the right and the west wing on the left. Part of a cruck barn can be seen on the extreme left.

posts, one authority believes timber framing was replaced by stone at some point after the erection of the building, while another believes the girding beams (timbers set horizontally at mid-wall height) have always rested on a wall of stone or cob. As a protection against damp, the principal posts all originally stood on stylobates, some of which can still be seen, and the lowest horizontal timbers (sill beams) rested on low stone walls.

A variety of patterns of timberwork was employed on Bishops' House. Herringbone patterns were employed on both wings, but that on the east wing points downwards and that on the west wing upwards. What is very noticeable everywhere on the building is that the timbers (studs) are closely spaced, with the spaces between them not much wider than the studs themselves. This close studding is a typical feature of timber-framed buildings in the north of England. The spaces between the studs in timber-framed buildings were filled with a variety of materials as already noted. At Bishops' House, split-oak laths were fixed horizontally into grooves cut into the sides of the studs, then covered with plaster.

Inside the house, notable features include the carpenter's numbering system carved into the first floor wall of the west wing, the adze marks on the shaped timber beside the stair head, the thick oak planks used to make the floors when upper rooms were put in the east wing in the seventeenth century, and the elaborately carved oak panelling of seventeenth-century date in the hall on the ground floor of the east wing.

Kirkstead Abbey Grange at Thorpe Hesley contains, in its roof, some of the most interesting carpentry of fifteenth- or sixteenth-century date in South Yorkshire. The building, so named when it was restored in 1900 by the earl of Effingham, was formerly known as Parkgate Farm. It is popularly thought to be a Norman building constructed in the second half of the twelfth century by the monks of Kirkstead Abbey in Lincolnshire, who had been given permission in 1161 by the lord of the manor to mine and smelt ironstone in Kimberworth township and to build a dwelling there. A detailed survey by the South Yorkshire County Archaeological Service in 1984 has shown that the building has a very complicated history and is late medieval rather than Norman, but incorporates stone and timber features from an earlier building, possibly the original one built by the Kirkstead monks in the late twelfth century.

Kirkstead Abbey Grange has a king-post roof. In this kind of roof, a series of king-posts rise from tie beams which rest on either timber-framed or, as in this case, stone walls. Rising from each end of the tie beams are principal rafters which are fitted into the top of the king-posts with mortise and tenon joints. Running from king-post to king-post and supported by braces are ridge pieces. Halfway down the principal rafters are purlins. This superstructure supports a large number of common rafters, running from the ridge piece to the top of the wall, which in turn support the roof covering, in this case sandstone slates.

In its original state the roof consisted of 212 timber components, all oak, including the shaped trunks of 183 individual trees. Most of it has survived, only rafters and purlins having been replaced in parts of the roof in the 1900 restoration and the more recent 1985 conversion. More than 84 per cent of the trees used were less than nine inches (23cm) in diameter, and only 11 per cent (the tie beams and the trees from

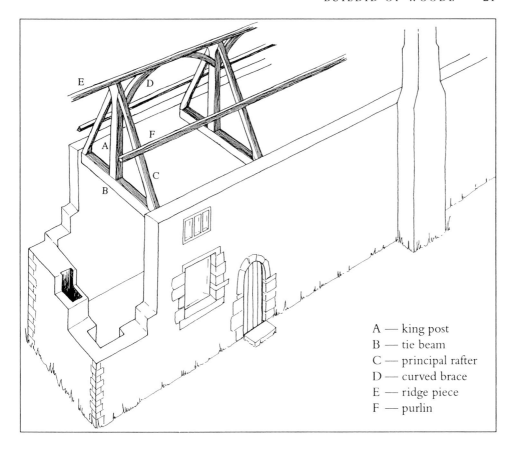

E
D
F
A
C
B

A — king post
B — tie beam
C — principal rafter
D — curved brace
E — ridge piece
F — purlin

The king-post roof structure at the southern end of Kirkstead Abbey Grange.

which the principal rafters were sawn) measure more than twelve inches (30cm) in diameter.

Detailed studies in East Anglia have shown that ordinary medieval buildings contain few timbers more than twenty feet (6m) long, and those that are longer are often crooked, knotty and tapering, showing that the carpenter was using every inch of the upper part of the trunk in order to gain extra length. At Kirkstead Abbey Grange, the tie beams are a little over eighteen feet (5.5m) long from wall to wall, so that, together with the ends that rest on the walls (about thirty-two inches (80cm) thick), they must be nearly twenty feet (6m) long. However, the tie beams are exceeded in length by one other member. The ridge piece extending northwards from the southern end of the roof is twenty-two feet (6.7m) long. At its northern end it is seven inches by seven inches (18cm x 18cm) in section, and this must represent the butt end (bottom) of the trunk, because it tapers southwards, gradually losing its square section and becoming waney (rounded at the corners through reaching the outside of the log). It was obviously important to fit together the individual ridge pieces so that they formed one continuous strong component running the whole length of the roof. The joint used in these circumstances was the scarf joint. The joint was originally held together by a vertical wooden key (now missing).

A number of other interesting and unusual aspects of the use of timber and the skills of the medieval carpenter can be illustrated by a closer inspection of the roof truss at Kirkstead Abbey Grange. The first thing to note is the tie beam. It is a knotty timber some fourteen inches by nine inches (36cm x 23cm) at its most massive central point, and it has a slight but obvious symmetrical curve or camber on its upper side. Its underside (called the soffit) is not curved but is decorated by a roll moulding running almost its entire length. At its eastern end the roll moulding ends in what are called beam stops. The king-post, which is seven feet (2.1m) high, is square for most of its length, but at the top it widens to form what are called jowls to make it easier to accommodate the heads of the principal rafters which are held in place by long wooden pegs called treenails. Treenails are used throughout the roof to secure joints, except where modern timbers have replaced the original ones. The principal rafters are interesting in that in section they are ten inches by five inches (25cm x 13cm), suggesting that they are a matching pair sawn from the same squared trunk which was originally ten inches by ten inches (25cm x 25cm). The trunk in fact must have been more massive than ten by ten inches at its butt end because, just before reaching the tie

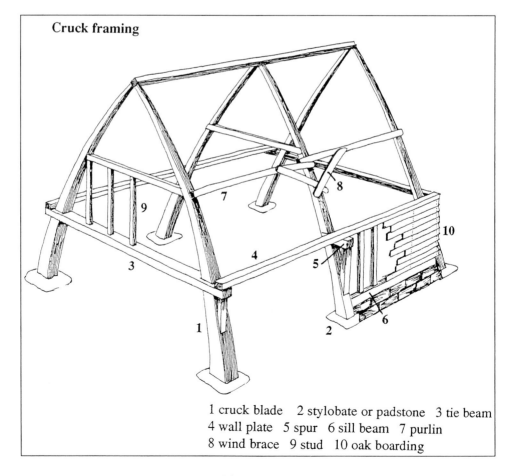

Cruck framing

1 cruck blade   2 stylobate or padstone   3 tie beam
4 wall plate   5 spur   6 sill beam   7 purlin
8 wind brace   9 stud   10 oak boarding

Constructional features of a cruck building.

Oaks Fold Barn, Shiregreen, Sheffield, looking west.

beam, the principal rafters develop broad shoulders which are quite unusual features. Originally, two matching curved braces from the king-post to the ridge piece helped to strengthen the truss, but only one has survived. The braces would have been specially shaped from naturally curving timbers. All the joints in the truss are mortise and tenon joints but the tenons are what are called barefaced tenons, that is the tenons have only one shoulder instead of the the usual two.

A final noteworthy feature of the truss is the numerical marking done by the carpenter. The truss would have been put together on the ground, perhaps on-site, or in the carpenter's yard or in a wood. Because there is evidence that much of the timber had been used in an earlier building, possibly one on the same site, the framework was probably put together on-site near to where the stone walls were being built. It was then marked with Roman numerals, knocked down, and then reassembled on top of the walls, using the marks to ensure that every part was in its correct place.

Cruck buildings are common in the upland areas of Britain and in parts of the Midlands but are virtually unknown in the east and south-east. Whether this indicates that they were never built there or were superseded at an early date by more sophisticated building methods is still an open question. In South Yorkshire there are only three records of cruck buildings in the area to the east of Rotherham, but to the west of the town there are records of nearly 150 cruck buildings either still standing or known to have been demolished since 1900.

In a cruck building, the weight is carried on pairs of timbers called cruck blades which rise from or near the ground and meet at the apex of the roof. The blades are usually curved, having been selected from naturally bent trees. Often a bent tree was

Close-up of cruck blade at Court House Antiques, Ecclesfield, showing where large branches have been sawn off the trunk of the tree.

split or sawn lengthways to make two matching blades. The structure is strengthened by tie beams connecting each pair of blades. If it was not convenient to have tie beams across the interior of the building, the wall plates were carried on spurs projecting from the back of a cruck blade and supported on a short vertical post. The roof of the building was stabilised by struts called windbraces. When such buildings had timber walls, the ends of the tie beams carried longitudinal wall plates. In the timber walls, vertical studs rose from sill beams to the wall plates. The gaps between the studs were filled with a variety of materials, as already noted, or alternatively the entire wall could be covered by horizontal oak boarding.

One of the best surviving cruck buildings in South Yorkshire is Oaks Fold Barn which stands at the entrance to Concord Park in Sheffield. It was described by John Harrison in his 1637 survey of the manor of Sheffield. He recorded 'ye tenement called Woolley Grange alias Oakes Farme with a dwellinghouse & a Barne of 5 bayes'. A bay is a space between each pair (in this case six) of cruck blades. Woolley Grange derives its name from the fact that it was originally a farm belonging to Ecclesfield Priory. The barn has long been encased in stone, and when that was done the wall plates became redundant and most were removed. Most of the windbraces have also disappeared. However, the cruck blades are on full view and at the far (west) end of the barn, some of the lath and plaster wall filling can still be seen.

Another cruck building that can be examined at very close quarters is the building housing Court House Antiques in Ecclesfield. The remarkable aspect of the cruck blades in this building is that in some cases it is possible to see where large branches have been sawn off the upper parts of the trunk of the trees.

'The Plucking Down of Religious Houses'

The Dissolution of the Region's Monasteries

As a boy of ten or eleven in the late 1940s, I took part in a cricket match at Monk Bretton cricket ground near Barnsley, the reason for which was not clear to me at the time. The two teams taking part were the Monks and the Cromwells. The thing that confused me was that the only Cromwell I knew about was Oliver Cromwell, and I couldn't see the connection between Oliver Cromwell and the monks of Monk Bretton Priory. The Cromwell in question, of course, was not Oliver Cromwell but Thomas Cromwell, one of Henry VIII's chief ministers and mastermind behind the scheme to make Henry the supreme head of the Church in England and to dissolve the monasteries.

Yorkshire had many monasteries and nunneries, and their dissolution had a big impact on the landscape and on ownership. Two questions that have always fascinated me are: how violent was the Dissolution? And what happened to the monks and nuns? Even though the events took place more than 450 years ago, some fascinating local evidence has survived.

Each monastic foundation in medieval Europe derived its ideal from the Rule of Benedict (c AD 480–547). Although rules differed in detail, all monks lived in communities, bound in obedience to the orders of the head of their establishment. They all took vows of celibacy and wore habits. As individuals they had little personal property. Each house maintained a daily cycle of prayer, usually on eight occasions, at regular intervals.

Monasteries were established in England and Wales from the sixth century onwards, but were almost extinct by the tenth century due to their destruction by the Vikings. The Norman Conquest inspired much expansion of the monastic life and monastic building. By the fourteenth century, monastic zeal was waning, and after the Black Death most monastic houses were half empty.

Many senior monks found themselves drawn into a very secular way of life of management and administration, and lived lives similar to country gentlemen. William More, prior of Worcester from 1518–36, had a day-book kept for him in which all the details of his receipts and expenses were kept. Purely by chance this journal has survived, and details from it are quoted in David Knowles' fascinating book *Bare Ruined Choirs*. Although not local, the life and preoccupations of the prior of Worcester give a very revealing insight into the life of a senior monk, the head of a wealthy house.

William More used an income equivalent to a quarter of the revenue of the abbey to maintain himself, a following of servants and four large manor houses. He lived the life of a country squire. In 1527–8 he only spent nine weeks at the priory. In his first year of office he spent £34 on carpentry work in his house at Crowle. At another house, Grimley, he spent money on the furnishings and decorations. In 1524–5 he had his Grimley home glazed from top to bottom with glass brought from London.

He was keenly interested in his deer park, fish ponds, rabbit warrens and dovecotes. There was expenditure on fencing, ditching, hunting and snaring. He often restocked the ponds and moats with tench, bream, eels, chub, roach, pike and carp and notes were made about the swans. No indication is given that the prior hunted although on one occasion he purchased a hunting horn for 3s 4d and three servants were provided with bows and arrows .

He also took part in large-scale entertainments on religious and other feast days. For example, in 1527 he paid 1s 4d to the girls at the village of Grimley for dancing for him on May Day. On another occasion the locals at Grimley performed a play based on the Robin Hood legend. Money was also paid to children who performed acrobatic tumbles, and to the king's juggler and his blind harper. He even bought himself a bag pipe. He also recorded gifts given to him on New Year's Day 1519 which included four dozen larks, two peacocks, one lamb, one pig, six snipe, a dish of trout, twenty oranges, and a silver and gilt garnished toothpick. William More's secular way of life — which also included giving and receiving presents from a 'lady' — was brought against him at the time of the Dissolution.

In the second half of the 1530s the monastic way of life, pious or not, came to a sudden end. In April 1536 there were more than 800 monasteries, nunneries and friaries in England and Wales with 10,000 inhabitants. By 1540 there were none. Yorkshire alone in 1536 had 34 monasteries, 23 nunneries and 19 friaries containing 610 monks, 230 nuns and about 200 friars. The friars were based in towns, unlike the monks in their rural solitude, and their purpose was to minister to ordinary people.

When the Dissolution began in 1536 it was presented as a reform. Smaller religious houses (ie those whose income was less than £200 per year) were closed initially in order that:

> the idle and dissolute monks and nuns who live in these dens of vice should be dispersed amongst the great abbeys, where they will, by discipline and example, be brought to mend their ways. The properties and endowments thus vacated can then be transferred to the king, to put to such better uses as he may think fit.

In Yorkshire in the smaller houses, 47 monks were accused of immoral relations with women, 9 were accused of homosexual practices and 92 were accused of self-abuse. Fourteen nuns were said to have borne children and another two had been 'unchaste'.

Henry's motive was not one of religious zeal but, most likely, to stave off the bankruptcy of the Crown. Thomas Cromwell and three assistants reported on every monastery and nunnery in a six-month period, and hardly a favourable word was said about them. Their visitations could hardly have been thorough. Monks and nuns were dispersed, servants paid off, goods and stock sold, and new lay occupiers became Crown agents. Precious metals, all altar furnishings and high-value items such as bells and roof-lead became the property of the Crown. Opposition came from the North with the uprising called the 'Pilgrimage of Grace' in October 1536 but the rebellion failed. The king crushed the participants without mercy. Ten Yorkshire monks were executed. In Lincolnshire the abbot of Kirkstead, who had various properties in South Yorkshire, was hanged.

From mid-1537 a second phase of Dissolution began, this time involving the great, rich abbeys. Cromwell sent his men on a new round of visitations, bullying and cajoling monasteries into handing over their properties. Excuses were found to prefer serious charges against any resilient abbot. By 1540 the Dissolution was complete.

It has to be said that as far as Yorkshire religious houses were concerned, the records show that, although there were some personal transgressions of vows, they were performing a useful function to the very end. James Aveling in his *History of Roche Abbey* published in 1870 reminds us that for centuries the monasteries were the keepers 'of the records of religion, philosophy and antiquity' and that the monks were:

> *lawyers, doctors, architects, chemists, artists, poets and practical farmers. In wild and solitary places they made roads, cut drains ... they entertained strangers and way-farers, and gave to the poor...*

All this had now gone.

Compensation was fair. Abbots and priors were often given generous pensions for life. The abbot at Roche Abbey, Henry Cundall, was granted an annual pension of £33, he was allowed to keep his books, a quarter of the abbey's plate, and 'the cattle and household stuff.' When the small houses were closed, monks and nuns could choose to be transferred to larger institutions or relinquish their vows.

Most of the great churches attached to the monasteries soon fell into decay. There was no general policy of destruction except in Lincolnshire. The buildings suffered from de-roofing and neglect with the locals taking stone for other buildings. At Monk Bretton, Thomas Wentworth bought the north aisle of the nave of the priory church with the pillars and arches to build a north aisle at Wentworth Church. A commissioner bought the site and sold it in 1589 to the earl of Shrewsbury, who gave it to his fourth son, Henry Talbot, on his marriage. Talbot adapted the prior's house into a residence.

Orderly dismantling of the buildings at Roche was planned, preceded by an auction. Before it could take place, however, a mob of local people descended on the abbey in a free-for-all of pillage. Movables went at once and some structures were pulled down. The church pews fuelled fires to melt the lead from the roofs. Michael Sherbrook, whose uncle was present at the dissolution of Roche, wrote in 1591: 'All things of price were either spoiled, carped away, or defaced to the uttermost...' Sherbrook's father bought timber stolen from the roof and steeple at Roche. When his son asked him how he could bring himself to do such a thing, he replied: 'What should I do? Might I not as well as others have some profit of the spoil of the abbey? For I did see all would away; and therefore I did as others did.'

Fortunately fourteen cathedral churches, formerly part of monasteries, survive in different parts of the country. Locally, the tower of the abbey church at Beauchief (then in Derbyshire) survived, as did most of the small priory at Ecclesfield. But as at Roche, only the ruins survive at Monk Bretton, and Hampole Nunnery has disappeared altogether.

Monk Betton Priory, looking from the kitchen towards the wall of the refectory with serving hatch.

The ruins of Roche Abbey.

The chapel and undercroft of Ecclesfield Priory, as portrayed in J Eastwood's *History of Ecclesfield* (1863).

The western tower of Beauchief Abbey, all that remains of the ecclesiastical and domestic buildings on the site. The attached chapel was built c1660. (Samuel Pegge, *An Historical Account of Beauchief Abbey*, 1801.)

Many monks found openings in the Church. Some became chantry priests (but chantries were dissolved in 1547). Chantries were private chapels, usually in parish churches, where masses for the soul of the founder or his nominees were held. Others became curates, vicars and rectors in the reformed Church. Substantial numbers married. Others went abroad (including to Scotland) to continue their former religious life. Others turned to secular vocations, particularly schoolmastering. Many simply retired and lived on their pensions — such as Henry Cundall, the ex-abbot of Roche, who lived with the vicar at Tickhill. It is said the large wooden chest in Tickhill Church belonged to Cundall who brought it with him from Roche. In his retirement he kept bees and made honey, and left two swarms of bees in his will to his godchildren. The thirteen monks and the prior from Monk Bretton Priory bought 148 books from the priory library and moved to Worsbrough where they continued to live together. Some monks died in poverty, their meagre pensions declining in value through inflation.

Nuns were less generously treated. Many had to depend on the charity of friends or relations — there were no career prospects for women then — and some married. Occasionally a few clung together to retain privately some semblance of their former community life. The longest known surviving monk or nun in Yorkshire was Isobel Coxson of Hampole Nunnery. She was twenty-two in 1536 when Hampole was dissolved and received a pension of £2 a year. She was still receiving it in 1602 when she was eighty-five years old.

Research suggests that the vast majority of monks and nuns were recruited locally, which would have made their re-absorption into the outside world easier than if they had come from a much wider area. Cistercian monks often took the name of their place of birth or last place of residence as their monastic surname. At Roche at the Dissolution there were monks named Cundall, Middleton, Drax, Dodworth, Helagh or Hylye (Heeley?) and Holand (Hoyland?).

'Halfway to the North Pole'
Sheffield in the Sixteenth and Seventeenth Centuries

'Halfway to the North Pole' is where Lord Lisle located Sheffield in a letter from Hampton Court to Gilbert, seventh earl of Shrewsbury, in 1606. But this perception of a place beyond the edge of the civilised world is scotched by John Harrison's remark in his survey of the manor of Sheffield in 1637 that 'this Mannor is not inferior to any Mannor in England…' Fortunately, there are a number of surviving documents that enable us to have a clear picture of the town in the second half of the sixteenth and the first half of the seventeenth centuries. The documents relate to the period when the fourth, fifth, sixth and seventh earls of Shrewsbury (1473 –1616) were lords of the manor, and to the early years of the time of the earl of Arundel and his wife Alethea (daughter and co-heiress of Gilbert, seventh earl of Shrewsbury). These documents reveal a small workaday market town within an aristocratic estate with its castle, country house and deer park.

The market town of Sheffield

The market town of Sheffield, which by the early seventeenth century had a population of about 3,000 and had twice-weekly markets on Tuesdays and Thursdays, grew up at the confluence of the rivers Don and Sheaf where the Norman lords, the de Lovetots, built a motte-and-bailey castle with a timber keep in the mid-twelfth century. The two rivers formed a natural moat on the north and east. This motte-and-bailey castle was destroyed by fire in the second half of the thirteenth century and replaced by a stone keep and bailey castle. This stone castle was 'sleighted and demolished' in the late 1640s following the Civil War and precise details of its layout have not survived, although excavations carried out in the 1920s revealed stretches of stone wall, a circular bastion next to the main gateway, and possibly part of the gatehouse and its drawbridge support. John Harrison in his 1637 survey said the castle was 'fairely built with stone & very spacious'. It comprised an inner courtyard bounded by 'a great ditch' round the western and southern sides with 'ye Great River of Doun lying on ye north parte thereof & ye Lesser River called ye Little Sheaf on ye east'. To the south of the moat was an outer courtyard containing 'an armory a Granary, Barnes Stables & divers Lodgeings'. This outer bailey is thought to have run south from the moat up the slope as far as the modern Fitzalan Square. Thomas Winder, who worked for many years in the duke of Norfolk's estate office in Sheffield, put together a sketch map of the castle site based on old maps he had consulted, reproduced opposite. The map shows a square hill on which the keep was located,

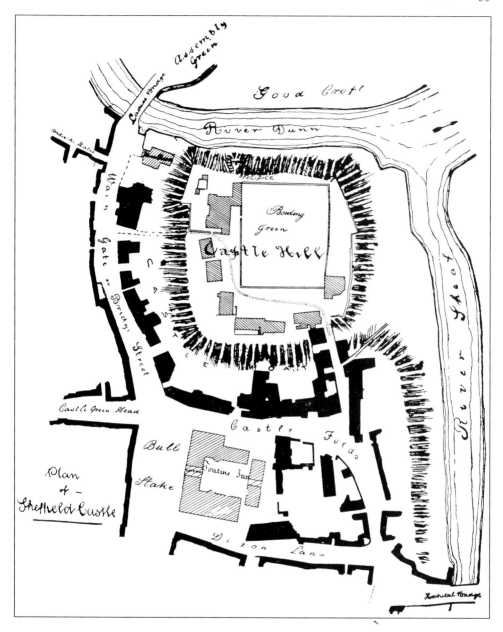

Thomas Winder's sketch map of Sheffield Castle.

the moat stretching south and east between the Don and Sheaf, and the close relationship between the keep and the entry into the town across the River Don via Lady's Bridge.

Outwardly forbidding, cold and probably draughty, the castle was not without its comforts in the Elizabethan period. An inventory of 1582 of the castle and the Manor Lodge (see below) lists a large number of wall hangings, including 'Forrest worke', 'ye storye of Hercules' and 'the storye of the Passion'. There were also various chimney hangings, and eight long and more than a dozen short 'Turkey carpetts'. The window curtains were of taffeta, silk, satin and buckram, and the coverings, curtains and counterpanes of the tester beds were of crimson and purple velvet, satin and silk, embroidered with silver and gold.

The market town of Sheffield grew up under the protection of the castle. Here in a tight cluster of narrow streets including Bridge Street (later renamed Waingate), Castle Green, Castle Folds, Dixon Lane, Water Lane, Snig Hill, Pudding Lane, Trueloves Gutter (also an open sewer) and Market Place lay the oldest part of the town. Contemporary documents give the impression of a tightly-knit collection of houses, cottages and outbuildings, mostly timber-framed, variously described in a rental of 1581 as 'a cottage with ii bayes', 'a house and Smethie', 'a cottage and garden', 'a house over and against Wm Heathcotes' and 'ii outshuttes joining to his house'. Intermingled among the cottages were 'swyne hulls' (pigsties), 'foldes' (small paddocks) and 'myddenstyds' (places for piling manure). This central area was also the most important part of the town's retail area, with shops spread in and around the 'Shambles House'. Here too was the market cross, and the bull stake where the town bull was tethered for hire. In nearby Pudding Lane was the public bakehouse where, as one of the paynes (byelaws) agreed by the jury at the court leet in 1609 stated, 'all the householders within the towne of Sheffield shall bake their Rye bread and wheate bread'.

The town spread out from this central core in every direction. To the east, Dixon Lane led to the River Sheaf where a stone bridge had been built in 1596 and which led to the Castle Orchards, on the southern edge of which in 1666, fifty years after his death, Gilbert, seventh earl of Shrewsbury's Hospital was erected for the housing of twenty-four poor townsfolk.

To the west and south-west, the town spread along High Street and Fargate, with houses occupying long 'burgage plots' (properties with frontages on busy streets belonging to burgesses — citizens or freemen of the town), separated in one or two places by long winding 'alleys'. At the junction of High Street and Church Street stood the town hall, a building erected on timber pillars, below which traders rented spaces, as in the case of Robert Bawre in 1581 who paid ten shillings 'for a shoppe under ye Court Chamber'. To the north of Church Street stood the medieval parish church (now the cathedral), with its Shrewsbury Chapel containing by the 1590s the tombs of George, fourth earl of Shrewsbury (1468–1538) and his two wives, and George, sixth earl (c1528–90). On the south side of Church Street from 1638 stood the Cutlers' Hall, the headquarters of the Cutlers' Company of Hallamshire, formed in 1624. At the far end of Church Lane stood the Townhead Cross and the Townhead Well.

Beyond the far end of Fargate was Balm Green, to the west of the present city hall, which contained Barkers Pool, a source of fresh water for the town's residents to supplement the town's public wells. In 1572 a stone wall was built round the pool and a shuttle or sluice gate fitted. Water from the pool was occasionally channelled through the town to clean its streets, eventually finding its way down Water Lane and along Trueloves Gutter into the River Don.

Northwards, beyond the Irish Cross, at the bottom end of Market Place, was Snig Hill, 'snig' thought to be the word for blocks of wood put through cartwheels to act as brakes, and as Snig Hill led to the town's manorial corn mill at Millsands, many a

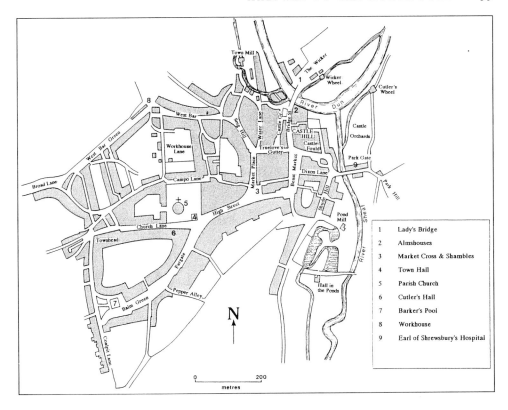

Sketch map of the town of Sheffield c1600.

1	Lady's Bridge
2	Almshouses
3	Market Cross & Shambles
4	Town Hall
5	Parish Church
6	Cutler's Hall
7	Barker's Pool
8	Workhouse
9	Earl of Shrewsbury's Hospital

heavy load must have had to be braked on the steep hill. Towards the bottom of Snig Hill came West Bar, a lane presumably leading to one of the gates into the Norman town; but this must remain a presumption as no other town entrance has survived as a local place-name. At West Bar stood the town's workhouse built in 1628 for poor children.

Lastly, the town extended across the River Don via the stone-built Lady's Bridge, constructed in 1486 to replace an earlier timber structure. Lady's Bridge was so called from the Chapel of Our Blessed Lady of the Bridge which stood to the south of the river under the castle walls. This chantry chapel, where travellers could pray for a safe journey, became disused after the Reformation, and had become a wool warehouse by 1572 and later became an almshouse for four poor people. It was rebuilt using stone from the demolished castle after the Civil War. North of Lady's Bridge, the road lay across a green called Sembly Green and the Wicker, leading to Spital Hill where William de Lovetot had built an isolation hospital (hence the name 'spital' which is simply a shortened version of 'hospital') outside the town in the twelfth century. On Sembly Green every Easter Tuesday the lord of the manor inspected the town's militia, consisting in 1637 of at least 139 men with 'Horse & Harnesse' for 'the Confirmeing of the Peace of our Soveraigne Lord the King'. On the Wicker were the town's archery butts and, until it was removed to Barkers Pool, a 'cucking-stool' for ducking nagging women and other objectionable persons.

The deer park

Coming right up to the western edge of the market town was the lord of the manor's deer park, which at its greatest extent covered 2,462 acres (997ha) and was eight miles (13km) in circumference. It had a typical shape, a rounded rectangle which was the most economic outline for fencing. By 1637 more than 971 acres (393ha) had been let to tenants, including the whole of the Little Park, all that part of the Great Park to the west of the River Sheaf, and all but two enclosures amounting to eighty acres (32ha) in the western third of the Great Park to the east of the Sheaf. The tenanted parts of the park in 1637 were a mixture of arable, grazing and meadow, but also included a coppice wood (Morton Bank). They also included Heeley Side, which was grazing land in which there were coal pits which Harrison said 'yieldeth great profit unto the Lord'. Two other enclosures within the tenanted parts of the park were the Quarries which were used to impound tenants' stray animals, and Rough Lees which were hay meadows 'for the deere and Mill horses'.

Those parts of the park still managed as a deer park in 1637 contained 1,000 fallow deer. These deer were obviously a temptation for certain sections of the population

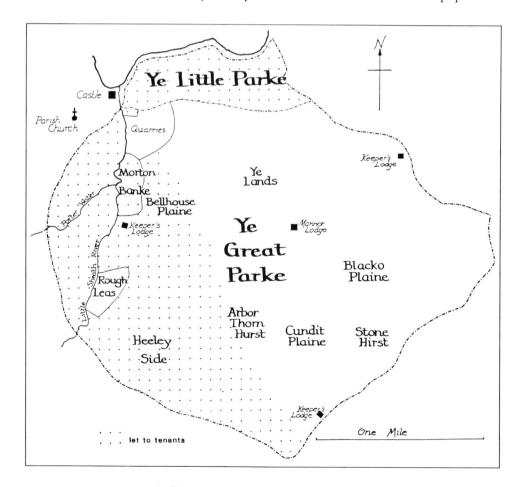

Sheffield deer park in 1637 (after G Scurfield).

The Turret House, Manor Lodge.

for, at the court leet of the manor of Sheffield in April 1578, six local men were each fined five shillings 'for huntinge the hare within my Lordes Parke ... to the disturbance of my Lordes game there, & killed one deare & dyd hyte an other deare'.

Harrison in his survey of 1637 names the various parts of the park, including some with woodland names such as Arbor Thorn Hirst and Stone Hirst (*hirst* was the name for a wooded hill), but these were probably only scrub woods. Other names, such as Ye Lands, Cundit Plaine, Blacko Plaine and Bellhouse Plaine suggest treeless areas. Ye Lands is probably a corruption of 'laund', a grassy treeless area in a deer park, and the word plain had a similar meaning. These treeless areas probably contained thickets of thorn and holly. They certainly contained scattered trees, pollarded to protect the regrowth. Some of these trees, most probably oaks, were described in some detail in John Evelyn's book *Silva or a Discourse of Forest Trees*, the first edition of which was published in 1667. For example, he described one tree in the park whose trunk was thirteen feet (4m) in diameter and another which was ten yards (9m) in diameter. On Conduit Plain (the 'Cundit Plaine' of Harrison's 1637 survey), Evelyn reported that there was one oak tree whose boughs were so far spreading that he estimated (giving all his calculations) that 251 horses could stand in its shade.

There were two important buildings standing in the original park. In the north-western corner, beside the ponds which by 1637 formed the water power for a second

Plaster ceiling in the second-floor room of the Turret House. The breed of dog is a 'talbot'.

lord of the manor's corn mill, stood the Hall in the Ponds. Dendrochronological analysis shows that this timber-framed building, which still survives in part, was built of timber felled between 1506–1510. It was probably a banquetting house for the lord of the manor and his guests used at the end of a day's hunting, fishing and fowling in the park.

On a much larger scale was the Manor Lodge, which was located near the centre of the park with glorious views in all directions. This was originally a hunting lodge, converted into a comfortable country residence by George, the fourth earl of Shrewsbury. Harrison in his survey of 1637 described it as 'being fairely built with stone & Timber with an Inward & an outward Court 2 Gardens & 3 Yards'. Mostly in ruins now, only the Turret House near the entrance to the site still survives largely intact. On the second floor is a room with an original Elizabethan fireplace and plaster ceiling. The Manor Lodge is famous because Mary, Queen of Scots, spent much time here during her long imprisonment under George, sixth earl of Shrewsbury.

Sheffield's royal prisoner

Mary, Queen of Scots, had sailed across the Solway Firth in May 1568 to exile in England following her defeat by the regent of Scotland after her escape from imprisonment because of her suspected involvement in the murder of her husband Lord Darnley and her destabilising influence on her country. Once in England she threw herself on the mercy of Queen Elizabeth, even though she had not relinquished her claim to the English throne. This put Elizabeth in a quandary. To allow Mary to remain in England meant that a claimant to the throne, and a Roman Catholic

Tomb of George, sixth earl of Shrewsbury (1468–1538) in the Shrewsbury Chapel
in Sheffield Cathedral.

The Hall in the Ponds.

claimant, was at large to plot and conspire; to escort her out of the country might re-invigorate a Franco–Scottish alliance; and to support her claim to the Scottish crown was likely to result in renewed political instability in Scotland. In the event, until her execution in 1587, Mary was held captive in England for eighteen years while Elizabeth pondered a resolution to the problem.

After a short stay at Carlisle Castle, Mary was brought south to Bolton Castle in Wensleydale and then to Tutbury Castle in Staffordshire and into the hands of George Talbot, sixth earl of Shrewsbury. The earl must have been seen by Queen Elizabeth as the ideal custodian for Mary. He was rich, he was powerful and his devotion to Elizabeth was beyond question. Moreover, he and his wife, the formidable Bess of Hardwick, owned vast estates with well-defended houses and castles, mostly off the main highways.

On the 28th November 1570 the earl safely delivered Mary to his stronghold at Sheffield Castle. She was to remain in captivity in Sheffield for fourteen years. The regime at the beginning of Mary's detention there was strict. Her retinue was reduced to thirty, none of her attendants could be with her after nine at night nor leave their sleeping quarters before six in the morning; and her servants, with the exception of her master of the household, were not to wear swords and none was allowed to leave the castle without the earl's permission. Mary herself had to give one hour's notice to the earl before leaving her private apartments, and then she was only allowed to walk on the 'leads' (the lead roofs) of the castle, in the dining chamber or in the castle yard, in the latter case only in the company of the earl or his wife.

Later the regime was relaxed somewhat and, with the exception of 1575, Mary spent part of every year between 1573 and 1584 at the Manor Lodge in the deer park. Moreover, because Mary's health was never good she was taken in summer to the country or for a health cure. She went on six visits to Chatsworth and a further six to the earl's spa house at Buxton.

All these changes of residence and prolonged health visits took place with great precautions and vigilance. Shrewsbury was instructed that they should be arranged with 'as little foreknowledge abroad as may be conveniently given' and Buxton was in a state of siege while Mary was there. There was even unease about her first move to the Manor Lodge, and Shrewsbury's son, Gilbert, had to assure Queen Elizabeth's close advisors that she was very closely guarded and 'unless she could transform herself to a flea or a mouse, it was impossible that she should escape'.

Two Planned Medieval Towns
Tickhill and Bawtry

Tickhill is one of the most attractive places in South Yorkshire. Despite the inevitable suburban expansion, the centre of the town still has the air of an ancient market town unaffected by industrialisation. This atmosphere is enhanced by the fact that the town centre has two rookeries, and the cawing of the rooks in spring, together with the carpets of celandines in the churchyard, give it a very traditional feel — what visitors from abroad expect a small English country town to be like.

Yet Tickhill did not grow naturally from an ancient village into a market town. It was an artificial foundation, a planned medieval town established by a Norman lord to serve his estate and his main residence — and for the modern visitor it is relatively easy to see how everything evolved.

The town Tickhill did not exist when the Domesday survey was carried out in 1086. The nearest place mentioned was Dadsley. It is not clear exactly where this settlement lay, as no signs have been found on the ground or through aerial photography. It was probably sited near Dadsley Well and Dadsley Lane about half a mile (0.8km) north of the town. A church existed to serve Dadsley and neighbouring settlements, and the site of this is at All Hallows Hill, again to the north of the present town.

Tickhill, which means Tica's Hill, came into existence sometime between 1086 and 1100 when the Norman lord, Roger de Busli, decided to build his castle there. De Busli had been granted extensive estates by William the Conqueror in South Yorkshire, Nottinghamshire, Derbyshire, Leicestershire and Lincolnshire. His South Yorkshire properties extended from Wentworth in the west to Barnby Dun in the east.

De Busli built a motte-and-bailey castle to establish his authority, to serve as the headquarters of his estates, and to defend an important south–north route from the East Midlands to the Tees. Tickhill Castle was part of a chain of Norman castles that controlled movement north towards Scotland on the eastern side of the Pennines.

De Busli's lands passed to Robert de Belleme, earl of Shrewsbury, but he backed a failed pretender to the English throne, and his castles including Tickhill were taken by King Henry I in 1102, and from then on Tickhill belonged to the Crown.

The castle was dominated by its motte, a hill seventy-five feet (23m) high and eighty feet (24m) in diameter, on which a timber and then an eleven-sided stone keep was built between 1178–82. Tica's Hill formed the bottom third of the motte, the rest being thrown up by Norman castle-builders. Below the motte was an elevated

Tickhill, looking north from Castlegate towards the eighteenth-century market cross.

Tickhill from the mill pond beside the castle, looking north towards St Mary's Church.

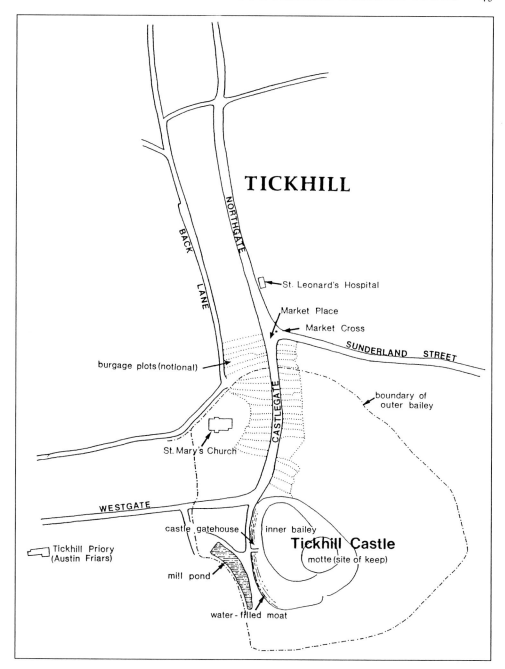

TICKHILL

St. Leonard's Hospital

Market Place

Market Cross

SUNDERLAND STREET

burgage plots (notional)

boundary of
outer bailey

NORTHGATE

BACK LANE

CASTLEGATE

St. Mary's Church

WESTGATE

Tickhill Priory
(Austin Friars)

castle gatehouse

inner bailey

Tickhill Castle

motte (site of keep)

mill pond

water-filled moat

Outline of medieval Tickhill.

defended area known as an inner bailey covering two acres (0.8ha), and bounded by a curtain wall and then surrounded by a water-filled moat.

The castle was the scene of a three-week siege in 1322 during a mini civil war, and it was the scene of action during the Civil War in the 1640s. After the defeat of the royalists in 1648, the keep was dismantled.

Although the motte and inner bailey are now private land, the visitor to Tickhill can walk round the western and southern boundaries, and see the water-filled moat, the remains of the curtain wall and gatehouse to the inner bailey, together with more distant views of the motte.

Encircling the inner bailey, and extending some distance to the east and north, was probably another defended space, the outer boundary of which was marked by a ditch whose location was identified during an excavation in 1975. This was the outer bailey. To the west this area contained a mill pond (still in existence) and to the east a deer park. To the north the outer bailey appears to have extended as far north as the market place, and to have included the parish church and churchyard within its boundaries.

Three of the four main streets in the defended medieval town are all called gates — Westgate, Castlegate and Northgate — betraying the Anglo-Norse language prevalent in this part of England at the time of the town's foundation. (*Gata* was the Old Norse word for a street or lane.)

The new town built under the protection of the castle was basically a one-street town, extending northwards from the eastern end of Westgate, up Castlegate to Northgate. The earliest town was probably restricted to Castlegate, with the market place at its northern end. Running off the central part of the market place eastwards is Sunderland Street. Sunderland means land 'put asunder' for a special purpose — possibly a market and fairground — Tickhill had a weekly market and annual fair from its foundation. Eventually the medieval town expanded westwards along Westgate, northwards along Northgate and eastwards along Sunderland Street. Only in the second half of the twentieth century has the old medieval town been surrounded by the usual outbreak of 'scarlatina' — red-brick suburbs that could be anywhere.

A feature of the original medieval town is that property boundaries run back from Castlegate and Northgate in the form of long narrow parcels. These are typical of medieval market towns and are called burgage plots, a burgage being the property held by a burgess (a property-holding town dweller). The reason that the burgage plots form long narrow parcels running back from the main streets is to enable the maximum number of tradesmen and craftsmen to have a street frontage to serve tenants coming to pay their rents, travellers moving north or south, and the rural population round about every market day. Significantly, in Tickhill, old maps show the burgage plots to be narrowest near the market place. An example of a long burgage plot can be seen by entering the coaching yard of the Red Lion Inn which has been turned into a specialised shopping area called St Mary's Court.

Worth seeing in the town are the market cross, which is not medieval but late eighteenth century; and St Leonard's Hospital, a timber-framed building dating from 1478, with an upper floor in mock medieval style rebuilt in 1851. St Leonard's Hospital, established in 1225, was originally a leper hospital.

The outstanding medieval structure in Tickhill is St Mary's parish church. Originally built in the thirteenth century to replace All Hallows at Dadsley, it was enlarged in the fourteenth and fifteenth centuries, and is one of the outstanding Perpendicular churches in South Yorkshire. It is built from Magnesian Limestone, and both inside and out can only be described as stately. It has a wonderful tower, 124 feet (38m) high with a figure in a niche on each of its four faces. Among the interesting items in the

General view of St Mary's Church, Tickhill, and its churchyard. The statues in their niches are important surviving features of the magnificent Perpendicular tower.

Pebbles in the nave wall of St Nicholas's Church, Thorne. The entire walls of the nave (including the clerestory) and the bottom stage of the tower are built mainly of pebbles.

Ecclesfield for example, wonderful examples of Perpendicular architecture. The last three churches mentioned — Laughton, Rotherham and Ecclesfield — all use different building stone. Laughton is of Magnesian Limestone (with an earlier church of sandstone embedded in the later one), Rotherham of Rotherham Red (Mexborough Sandstone), while Ecclesfield under its grime is built of a much paler, yellowy-cream Coal Measure sandstone.

The stonework is usually in the form of beautifully worked blocks called ashlar (as opposed to roughly worked stone called rubble). The church at Burghwallis north of Doncaster is made of rubble but the stones are beautifully arranged in a herringbone pattern — which usually denotes a Saxon period building. In the eastern part of the county beyond Doncaster, stone had to be transported in by water and was expensive. As a result, some churches used large amounts of pebbles, deposited by ice and water and picked from ditches, fields and riverbeds as the churches were being constructed. Large amounts of pebbles were used in building the churches at Kirk Sandall, Fishlake, Hatfield and particularly Thorne.

Church exteriors also need to be searched carefully for gargoyles decorating the ends of water spouts, often in animal and grotesque form. Those at Bradfield, Ecclesfield and Silkstone are worth careful scrutiny. Church towers often contain interesting clocks and sundials. Many churches had a niche on the tower for a small statue of its patron saint, but most were removed at the Reformation. The niches at Tickhill still have their statues, the one on the eastern side being of St Mary to whom

Elaborate medieval door-hinges on the south door of St Helen's Church, Burghwallis.

Fifteenth-century stained-glass window at St Leonard's Church, Thrybergh.

the church is dedicated. A most unusual tower feature is to be found at Royston — an oriel window (a window projecting from the second storey supported on brackets).

Some churches have interesting porches. There is a fine one at Worsbrough. The one at Thorpe Salvin is a rare half-timbered one. And the walls of the one at Tankersley are lined by broken slabs incised with crosses and swords.

And last, before you go inside, have a good look at the doorway and the door. There are three particularly good Norman doorways in South Yorkshire at Thorpe Salvin, Fishlake and Austerfield. The door arch at Fishlake has several semi-circular rows of intricate carving of figures, faces and leaves — the most lavishly decorated doorway in Yorkshire. The one at Austerfield goes one better than Fishlake: the archway is again decorated with a pattern of zigzag and beak carving, and then the semi-circular space above the door — the tympanum — is filled with the carved figure of a dragon. And there may be a medieval door with its elaborate medieval door hinges, as at Burghwallis and Hooton Pagnell.

The church interior

Once you're in the church, I can't improve on the advice given by Frank Bottomley in his book *Yorkshire Churches*: go to the back of the church and look at the overall character and structure. Some are simple, solid and strong such as Conisbrough, large parts of which are Saxon; others are light and airy such as Rotherham and Ecclesfield.

Churches are made up of two or three basic compartments and the rest is just elaboration. The main compartment is the nave, which is the main 'room' you see from

The tympanum of the Norman doorway at St Helena's Church, Austerfield, with its carved figure of a dragon.

The magnificent carved Norman font at St Peter's Church, Thorpe Salvin,
showing the scene of a baptism.

the back of the church. Beyond that is the chancel. The nave is for the congregation and the chancel is for the clergy. Behind you there may be the third compartment — the tower. The rest, such as aisles in the nave and side chapels, is just elaboration on the basic plan.

Some churches have a cruciform plan, as at Rotherham, in which the nave and chancel form the upright part of the cross and the arms of the cross are made up of transepts on either side. A tower was often built where the four arms of the cruciform met, again as at Rotherham.

Near you, at the back of the church, will be the font. This is the most important item of nave architecture, often retained through several church rebuildings and so is often the oldest item in the church. Among Norman fonts, two of the best are in Rotherham parish church and at Thorpe Salvin, the latter having magnificent carvings of the seasons of the year and of a baptism. Fonts and font covers were often smashed by Puritan reformers, so a number of South Yorkshire's medieval churches have seventeenth-century replacements.

Magnificent features in many parish churches are their windows of stained glass. Glass is fragile and much medieval work has been lost. At Ecclesfield it is known that there were stained-glass windows showing the deer keepers of Rivelin and Loxley but these have gone. Some of the best medieval stained glass survives at Thrybergh, where one window shows a male member of the Reresby family kneeling at a shrine and another of a kneeling lady, probably another member of the Reresby family. They are of fifteenth-century date. There is some interesting nineteenth-century stained glass in local churches: for example, a window dedicated to Mrs Margaret Gatty at Ecclesfield and a Burne Jones window at Tankersley. Some of the most ambitious stained glass of all is early twentieth century, and illustrates the history of Sheffield and surrounding district in the chapter house in Sheffield Cathedral. It is by Christopher Webb (born 1866). Scenes portrayed include the monks making iron at Kimberworth in 1161, Mary Queen of Scots and her secretary, John Wesley preaching, and Huntsman and his crucible steel process.

Eyes need to be raised to the roof. Our ancestors made good use of local timber to create long-lasting roofs which they carved and painted. The best local roof is probably the one in the nave at Rotherham. There is another fine one with carved bosses in the Blythe chapel at Norton.

There are some good examples of early pulpits surviving in our local churches at the far end of the nave. There is an exceptionally ornate one at Rossington. Of later examples, the early seventeenth century one at Rotherham is worth going to see. And look out for the lectern, holding a large Bible for readings. A favourite design is a brass eagle with its outstretched wings holding the good book.

The boundary between the nave and chancel in a pre-Reformation parish church was in the form of a wooden screen called a rood screen. There are good surviving rood screens at Burghwallis, Campsall, Ecclesfield, Owston and Hatfield.

Once into the chancel, the visitor needs to look for early seating arrangements for the clergy and the choir. Look for misericords, seats that could be used during long services and gave the appearance that the person was standing and not sitting. The supporting bracket was often elaborately carved. Misericords survive at Rotherham,

Early fourteenth-century oak knight at St Peter's
Church, Barnburgh. He is holding his heart in

Ecclesfield, Loversall and Sprotbrough. On a smaller scale but still using local timber are the decorations on the bench ends (called poppy heads) in the chancel — particularly good are the ones at Rotherham and at Ecclesfield (one shows Mary carrying the baby Jesus, and another St Catherine with her wheel), which may have been done by the same craftsman.

The vicinity of the medieval altar was often provided with stone seats (called sedilia) for the clergy. Good examples survive at Burghwallis, South Anston and Thorpe Salvin. Look out also for a piscina, a small bowl with a hole in the middle for the disposal of holy water, usually set in the wall. Good examples survive at Conisbrough, South Anston and Sprotbrough.

Throughout the church are likely to be found memorials to individuals, families and larger groups of people. They are in various forms: brasses, incised slabs, effigies and hanging wall monuments. Fine examples of incised slabs can be found at Thorpe Salvin (figure of Katherine Sandford, c1461) and at Thrybergh (figure of Arnold Reresby, c1485).

Brasses are not common in South Yorkshire. Ones to see are the memorial to the Swift family in Rotherham parish church (1561); to Thomas Gascoigne (1556) at Burghwallis; to William Fitzwilliam and his wife at Sprotbrough (1474); and to John Morewood (died 1647) at Bradfield.

Effigies are the most elaborate medieval memorials. In South Yorkshire it is worth going to see the medieval knight carved out of oak at Barnburgh. Another carved effigial monument (a double-decker monument) can be seen at Worsbrough. Fine examples of effigies in stone can be seen at Treeton (knight in chain mail); South Anston (male adult and child); Wentworth old church (Sir Thomas Wentworth, died 1588, and his wife Margaret); Sheffield Cathedral (fourth and sixth earls of Shrewsbury); and Ecclesfield (Sir Richard Scott, died 1638). Among the best hanging wall monuments are the ones at Wentworth old church to Sir William Wentworth (died 1614) and his wife Anna (died 1611); to Henry Sandford (died 1582) and his wife Margaret at Thorpe Salvin; and to Lionel Reresby (died 1587) at Thrybergh.

'Leasing, Building and Baptising'
The Aristocratic Owners of Wentworth Woodhouse

Aristocratic and gentry landowners were and still are fastidious keepers of records: of inherited landownership and land acquisitions by purchase and judicious marriage; of rental agreements and rent collection; of outgoings and income; of building projects large and small; the list is almost endless and the detail is almost unbelievable.

And nearly all records, up to the beginning of the twentieth century at least, are available for scrutiny in record offices. In Sheffield Archives, for example, the largest record office in South Yorkshire, are deposited the estate records (and in some cases personal papers) of such important local families as the Spencer-Stanhopes of Cannon Hall, the Vernon-Wentworths of Wentworth Castle and the Wortleys of Wortley Hall (called the Wharncliffe Muniments); and, most importantly, of the dukes of Norfolk and their predecessors, the largest landlords in the Sheffield area (the Arundel Castle Manuscripts), and of the Wentworths, Watson-Wentworths and Wentworth-Fitzwilliams of Wentworth Woodhouse (the Wentworth Woodhouse Muniments). And of course, for more recent times, estate records and personal papers are supplemented by press coverage and the work of local photographers.

What is attempted here are just three glimpses into the lives, concerns and preoccupations of three heads of the families that owned the Wentworth Woodhouse estate, using estate and other local records.

Thomas Watson-Wentworth visits his Irish estates in 1713

The first glimpse, which is based entirely on accounts kept by the family's Irish agent, concerns 'His Honour' (as he was called) Thomas Watson-Wentworth, who inherited the Wentworth estate in 1695.

Thomas Watson-Wentworth (1665–1723) was the third son of Edward Watson, second baron of Rockingham of Rockingham Castle in Northamptonshire. His mother, lady Rockingham, was Anne Wentworth (1627–1696), daughter of Thomas Wentworth, first earl of Strafford (1593–1641) and sister of William Wentworth, second earl of Strafford. When the second earl of Strafford died childless in 1695, his will named his nephew, Thomas Watson of Rockingham Castle, as his sole heir. Thomas Watson added Wentworth to his name as the second earl of Strafford's will stipulated, took up residence at Wentworth Woodhouse (which he usually referred to simply as Wentworth House) with his wife Alice, and devoted himself not only to the management but also the expansion of his estates.

His inherited estates were extensive. In South Yorkshire was a compact estate of over 9,000 acres (3,650ha). He also inherited a vast acreage of estates in Ireland which had been acquired by his great-uncle, the first earl of Strafford, who had been lord lieutenant (viceroy) of Ireland from 1633–9. During that time the first earl had obtained from the Crown small estates on the coast of County Wicklow at Newcastle and Wicklow town, and had purchased another small estate around the town of Naas in county Kildare, and large ones in south-west County Wicklow at Shillelagh and Cashaw.

Altogether, the Irish estates covered a staggering 90,000 acres (36,500ha). To put the importance of the Irish estates into their overall context, in 1723, the year in which Thomas Watson-Wentworth died, the income from all his properties (including purchased properties in North Yorkshire and Northamptonshire) amounted to about £16,000. Of that more than £6,000 accrued from his Irish estates — ie thirty-eight per cent of his entire annual income.

In the case of his South Yorkshire estates, he kept a close eye on day-to-day estate management. This was not possible in the case of the Irish estates. There he was an absentee landlord and the Irish estates had to be left in the hands of land agents whose responsibilities included dealing with tenants, collecting rents, overseeing the management of woods, and taking money to Dublin and arranging its transfer to England.

The one aspect of the management of the Irish estates that demanded the personal attention of Thomas Watson-Wentworth was leasing policy. What must be remembered was that Ireland in the early eighteenth century was an English colonial possession and one in which the native Irish Roman Catholic population was regarded as disloyal to the Crown, and was subject to a number of penal laws. Within their estates, Protestant landowners such as Thomas Watson-Wentworth were determined to settle or 'plant' a Protestant (mainly English and mainly Anglican) chief tenantry loyal to the Crown: chief tenants were subject to written leases from the landlord, but usually leased portions of their tenanted land to sub-tenants. A substantial number of leases were coming to the end of their term in 1713 and Thomas Watson-Wentworth needed to discuss these with his land agents before renewing them. He also wished to ensure that his Irish woods were being managed as he had instructed. A visit to his Irish estates was called for.

He probably left Wentworth House towards the end of the second week in August 1713. With him were a number of servants who were to accompany him to Ireland, together with others who were making the journey to the port of embarkation and then returning to Wentworth. They were probably in charge of a coach which contained enough luggage for a protracted stay. He even took his own riding horses with him. It was via the Dee at or near Chester that he boarded ship. His route over the Pennines to the west coast must remain a mystery; no records have survived. The journey to the Dee would have taken about three days with two overnight stops.

The ship to Ireland would, of course, have been a sailing ship, so that the date of sailing, and the duration of the journey and the date of arrival, would only be known approximately. This is borne out by a number of entries in the principal agent's

Captain Nickson awaiting the arrival of Thomas Watson-Wentworth.

accounts itemising his expenses as he waited for his employer ('my master' or 'his Honour') to arrive. The principal agent's name was Captain Abraham Nickson who resided in the 'big house' at Coolattin near Shillelagh in the middle of the Wicklow estate. He rode to Dublin and on the 16th August and hired a coach, 'him goieing to Rings End to meet his Hon'. Ringsend was the port area for Dublin. The ship had not yet arrived. Thomas Watson-Wentworth did not arrive until the 25th August. Nickson had had to wait for ten days. He recorded in his accounts that he paid 'the Sea Men yt slung his Honrs Horses to shore' and for the hire of a Ringsend car to carry his employer's 'Portmantle Sadles etc'. He also paid for a load of straw and two barrels of white oats for the horses.

Nickson had taken lodgings for Thomas Watson-Wentworth and his servants. Having installed them in their lodgings, he arranged for copies of the Irish estate papers to be brought from two secure rooms where they were permanently stored.

In the meantime, four other trusted estate employees arrived in Dublin carrying more than £600. On such trips, these men were usually heavily armed. In 1708 Nickson had recorded in his accounts that on one particular trip from Coolattin to Dublin he had been carrying 'a considerable Sume of my Masters Moneys', and had

Thomas Watson-Wentworth (1665–1723).

been accompanied by four companions, 'there being a Man killed on ye Rode a few days before'. He also recorded in 1712 a payment 'for Mending a double barreld Carbine In ordr to Guard ye moneys'.

This armed party then provided the escort for Thomas Watson-Wentworth when he set off to 'view his estate'. About twelve in number, they must have formed a colourful and purposeful group. They went south-west out of Dublin, skirting the northern fringes of the Wicklow Mountains. Thomas Watson-Wentworth would have stayed at Abraham Nickson's old house, set in a park near to what was to become the main estate village, Shillelagh. There would also have been a new house to be seen in the course of construction. Nickson recorded that he was building 'a New house at Coolattin adjoyning to the old House' in 1711. Watson-Wentworth gave Nickson £100 towards the building costs in that year. The park at Coolattin also contained the famous Shillelagh oaks, of which there were more than 2,000 in 1728, valued at more than £8,000 and described as 'The Glory and ornament of the Kingdom of Ireland'.

The rest of September, Thomas Watson-Wentworth was based at Coolattin, no doubt inspecting farms and woods. On the 11th September he was at the outlying property at Toorboy, high in the Wicklow Mountains at nearly 2,000 feet (610m). On the 18th September the party moved on to the smaller properties at and around Wicklow town, Newcastle and Rathdrum, and thence back to Dublin.

The rest of Thomas Watson-Wentworth's stay in Ireland seems to have been restricted to Dublin, with Abraham Nickson moving between the capital and the Wicklow estate. The drawing up and signing of new leases, and meeting some of his grander tenants who rented large acreages, and who were not only part of the country gentry but spent part of the year in Dublin, would have occupied some of his time. He would also no doubt have taken part in the social and cultural life of Dublin.

It is interesting to note that, during his stay in the capital, Nickson arranged for his master to taste Ireland's unique drink and to see an animal long extinct in England. On the 13th October he noted a payment to 'a Man yt fetched a vessel of Usquebagh from Drogheda for his Honor'. *Usquebagh* was of course the Gaelic for 'water of life', in other words Irish whiskey. Then on the 28th October he paid 'Dennis Duiggen for bringing ye Wolf whelp from Collattin to Dub. for his Honr'. Wolves had been extinct in England since the late fourteenth century and they were on the verge of extinction in Ireland.

The final record of his stay in Ireland was on the 11th November when Abraham Nickson recorded that he was due 'to Imbarque for England'.

Thomas Watson-Wentworth's 1713 visit to his Irish estates was one of only two that he undertook between inheriting his uncle's estates in 1695 and his death in 1723. These two visits were crucial in setting and maintaining the estate policy that was to ensure a substantial and steady income from Ireland during the rest of the eighteenth century, an income that was to make a major contribution to the purchasing and building policy of Thomas Watson-Wentworth, and his son and grandson, the first and second marquises of Rockingham. Between them, these three heads of the Watson-Wentworth dynasty doubled the size of the South Yorkshire estate from 9,000 to about 18,000 acres (7,300ha) between 1695 and 1782. They also built the mansion at Wentworth Woodhouse that we see today, one of the largest Palladian mansions in England.

The first marquis of Rockingham's 'remarks and observations'

The next glimpse into the lives of the owners of the Wentworth estate concerns the son of the Hon Thomas Watson-Wentworth, also called Thomas Watson-Wentworth (1695–1750). He succeeded to the estate on the death of his father in 1723. He was a strong supporter of the Hanoverian succession and was the organiser of Whig power in Yorkshire. His support for the Whig cause and later his role in the suppression of the 1745 Jacobite rebellion brought him a succession of honours. In 1728 he was created baron Wentworth of Malton, and in 1734 baron of Harrowden and viscount Higham of Higham Ferrers, and baron of Wath and earl of Malton. In 1745, on the death of his cousin Thomas Watson, third earl of Rockingham, he succeeded to the barony of Rockingam (the earldom ceasing to exist). Finally, in 1746 he was created marquis of Rockingham.

Soon after coming into his inheritance, the future first marquis of Rockingham arranged for the details of his estate to be set out in a large volume of some 130 leaves of vellum, bound in the same material and secured by two metal clasps. The volume seems to have begun as a record of manorial courts in 1654. The book was then turned round and the rental details of the future marquis's estate begun at the other end. (It is now part of the Wentworth Woodhouse Muniments in Sheffield Archives.) Interesting and important as the rental details are, giving a detailed summary of his landed inheritance, the volume's over-riding interest lies in the fact that the marquis used the volume to record, in his own hand, what are called on the back cover 'many remarks & observations…' from 1724 almost until the day he died in 1750.

The marquis had much to say about his children in his rent roll book. For five of them — Anne (born 1722, and who married earl Fitzwilliam in 1744), Mary (born 1727), William (born 1728), Charlotte (born 1732) and Henrietta Alicia (born 1737) — he compiled a list not only giving their exact dates of birth but also their (mostly aristocratic) godparents. The other children to whom he refers were Thomas (born 1720) and Charles, the future second marquis of Rockingham, (born 1730).

On the 9th January 1733, which was Thomas's birthday, he gave a large party at Wentworth Woodhouse. The party had a double significance because it also marked the near completion of his new Baroque mansion (see pages 72-73). He described how the food was laid out in the dining room, prayer room, old laundry, old store room and old kitchen. All the guests had tickets telling them 'which room to repair to'. Men and women were separated, and they were taken to 'the best Rooms & the Inferior according to their Rank'. He then goes on to list all the dishes that were served — 225 in all — comprising 'of beef 43, of Pork 30, Venison Pastys 24, Turkeys 15, Geese 21, Puddings 30, Apple or minced Pyes 16, Fowls 14, Boar's Heads 4, Mutton 28, one hundred sixpenny loaves of White Bread, about eight Hogsheads of Ale and three of small Beer, twelve Dozen of Wine and Two Hogsheads of Punch.'

Unfortunately, one guest died: 'a too melancholy thing happened, a poor man dyed, as supposed by a Fall, in the Courtyard being in Liquor'.

He also recorded the deaths of his sons Thomas and William. Thomas 'dyed of the Small Pox at Leyden' on the 14th August 1734. The fourteenth day of August was a generally unlucky day for the Watson-Wentworths, as the marquis related:

> ... the same day was very remarkable to my present Eldest Son William. On 14 August he fell into the Bason in the Garden when no Body but a Boy was by, who providentially helped him out else he had probably been drowned being very young & on 14 August 1732 as he hastily shut a Door, a large Picture which hung over it fell down with that violence as to shatter the frame to pieces & by God's providence fell over the child so as he remained unhurt between the Door and the Picture.

William only survived until 1739, the marquis recording his early death, aged eleven, 'after a Feaverish Illness of about a month's continuance dyed at Hampstead.'

William's death and the earlier death of Thomas gave the marquis pause for thought at the end of 1739:

> ... so that this Unfortunate Year when I lost my Dear Eldest Son William Lord Higham for whom I hoped to have prepared these Conveniencys [ie his new mansion at Wentworth Woodhouse] I had laid out in the whole as near as I could compute fifty six thousand pound — God prevent our being attached to the Honours Grandeur or State of the World above what we ought, & Bless my now Dear & only son Charles to a long and Christian Life to the enjoyment of these so as to be fit at leaving them to enjoy Everlasting Glory.

The future marquis had started building a new mansion in the Baroque style facing west in 1724, but before he had finished building and furnishing it (in 1734), he had already commenced the erection of another, bigger house, in the Palladian style and facing east. It is this latter mansion, which was not completed until after his death, that we are familiar with today.

He meticulously recorded progress, setbacks and expenditure on his building projects. He computed that the outlay on building work between 1722 and 1733 was more than £27,000. By the spring of 1736, building expenditure had risen to more than £36,000 and included the building of part of the east front '7 windows in length'. By 1738 the great hall of the east front was built and covered, and the 'supping room' finished. In 1739 the 'great porticoe' of the east front was complete By the spring of 1739 his building expenditure at Wentworth had risen to £56,800, and by 1744, by which time he was buying Cumberland slate for the main roof, it was £74,000. By 1748 he was able to record that there was 'nothing but Furnishing, Finishing and Levelling' to be done. At the end of that year his total building expenses had reached an astonishing £86,000, including £3,500 for 'Statues bought ... by Ld Malton [the future second marquis] at Rome and other places'. By the time the first marquis died in 1750, the building expenses had reached £90,000.

The expenses itemised above had been incurred not just on building one mansion and then another, but also in laying out and furnishing the pleasure grounds

Wentworth Woodhouse: the westward-facing Baroque mansion.

immediately around the house(s) and the park beyond. He recorded the completion of a ha-ha (hidden barrier ditch) and the setting up of obelisks in the garden in 1729, and in 1732 a keeper's lodge, park wall, a greenhouse and an obelisk in Lee Wood are mentioned. In 1735 and 1736 the 'Terrass' was made, and an ice house and 'The Tempiatto' built. The terrace which stretched westwards for 500 yards (450m) from the southern end of the Palladian mansion was flanked by a bastion wall which collapsed and had to be rebuilt. Both the terrace and the bastion wall survive to the present day.

Outside the park, on one of the highest points in the estate, he built Hoober Stand. This 'Pyramidal Building', as he called it, was begun in 1747 in honour of King George II and the suppression of the 1745 Jacobite rebellion. His son Charles, the future second marquis, at the age of fifteen had run away and joined the the king's army under the duke of Cumberland. The monument was probably also built in relief at the safe return of his only surviving son and heir.

At the same time that he was laying out the park and embellishing it with monuments, he was also extending it. In the early 1740s he wrote that:

> The Totall Circumference of the whole Park at Wentworth House, following the Angles of the Wall & including Scholes Wood & the new Park viz Greasborough Common is six miles & seventeen Hundred & twenty two yards that is nearly seven Miles.

By 1744 the park was more than nine miles (14km) in circumference.

The marquis also recorded some interesting details about his fruit growing. He seems to have started to cultivate pineapples in his heated greenhouses or 'stoves' at Wentworth in 1737, stating that they were then 'very scarce in England.' By 1740 he noted that he had got their cultivation 'to great perfection' and had produced one that weighed 3½ lb (1.6kg) which was '20 inches in girth the long way round and 16 inches the other'. In 1745 he says he had cut more than 200, sometimes as many as sixteen a day.

He also cultivated grapes, 'Sweet water or Early Grapes' but also 'Hambergh and Frontiniak'. He noted that in April 1746:

> I presented His Majesty with one Bunch of Frontiniak Grapes & one of Muscadine perfectly ripe, which He eat the Day after He Received the news of the Dukes Victory over The Rebells in Scotland.

It is unusual to be able to get a clear picture of a great country estate at a particular period from just one source, and this is what makes the first marquis of Rockingham's rent roll book so interesting. The combined force of the formal rental entries, together with his own informal records, observations and marginal notes, makes this a unique document, and provides a real insight into his preoccupation with his estate and its enlargement and embellishment, his political leanings, and his dynastic and personal preoccupations. But it is his estate that lies at the centre of his concerns. Let the first marquis have the last word. In 1750, the year of his death, in a letter to his son Charles, the future second marquis and prime minister (twice), he said: 'If you lay out your money in improving your seat, land, gardens, etc, you beautifye the country and do the work ordered by God himself'.

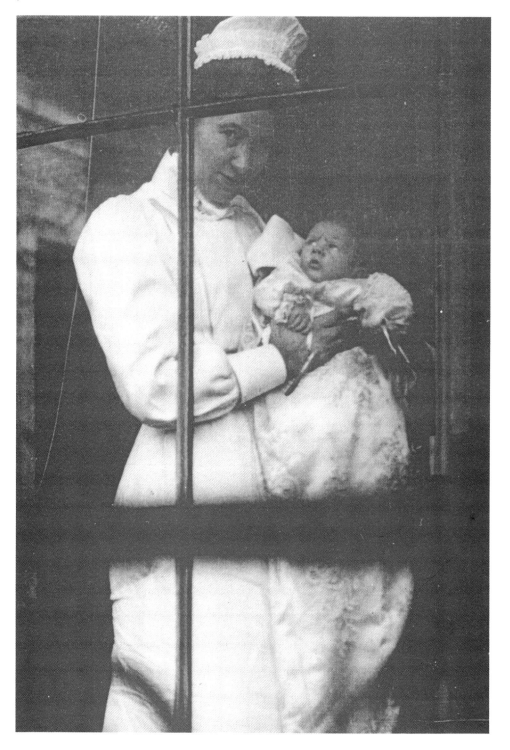

Viscount Milton being displayed on christening day.

Viscount Milton's christening in 1911

The third and final glimpse into the lives of the owners of Wentworth Woodhouse brings us into the early years of the twentieth century. The occupier then was the seventh earl Fitzwilliam. The Fitzwilliams had inherited Wentworth Woodhouse and its estates in 1782 when the second marquis of Rockingham had died childless. The first Fitzwilliam inheritor was the second marquis's nephew, the fourth earl Fitzwilliam.

The seventh earl's first four children were all girls. It had begun to be feared that the earldom — which, of course, could only be inherited by a male heir — would go to another branch of the family. The heir presumptive, before the birth in December 1910 of viscount Milton (this was the courtesy title used by the heir to the earldom), was the seventh earl's uncle, the Hon William Henry Fitzwilliam, who was seventy years old. The christening, therefore, was not just the celebration of a new life but a relief that the earldom would stay in the immediate family.

For this reason the event took on the characteristics of a coronation. Seven thousand official invitations were sent out, and for the day of the christening (Saturday the 11th February) the whole of the grounds was thrown open to the public and between 50–100,000 were expected to turn up.

A representative of the miners of Elsecar Main and New Stubbin collieries presenting a christening bowl to earl and countess Fitzwilliam.

The *Rotherham Advertiser* did not think the estimate was an extravagant one in view of the earl's popularity throughout South Yorkshire. He was not only an important landlord but a very significant employer, and his influence directly and indirectly on people's lives for many miles around was immense. There are still a few people alive who attended the christening.

The christening took place at one o'clock in the private chapel in the mansion. The service was conducted by the Rev R E W Verini, vicar of Wentworth and the earl's private chaplain. The event was attended by just the family and relatives. Viscount Milton was christened William Henry Lawrence Peter. The Hon William Henry Fitzwilliam and the marquis of Zetland (father of countess Fitzwilliam) were the godfathers, and the duchess of Buccleuch was the godmother.

A special feature of the christening was that a scarf which William the Conqueror was alleged to have taken from his arm at the Battle of Hastings, and handed to an ancestor of the seventh earl in recognition of his service and valour, was used to wrap the baby. This was a longstanding Fitzwilliam tradition, last used when the seventh earl was baptised.

To coincide with the birth of the male heir, a special brew of ale had been made by Whitworth, Son and Nephew of Wath upon Dearne. 'A tremendous number of hogsheads', to quote the *Rotherham Advertiser*, had been delivered to the vaults at Wentworth Woodhouse, where they would sit for twenty-one years years and then be consumed on the viscount's coming-of-age in 1931.

After the christening ceremony, at about two clock, a series of presentations took place on the steps in front of the mansion. A two-handled inscribed silver bowl was

Wentworth Woodhouse: the eastward-facing Palladian mansion.

The firework display at the christening of Viscount Milton.

presented to the earl and countess for the infant heir from the earl's tenants at Greasbrough, Rawmarsh, Upper Haugh, Thorpe Hesley and Scholes; another was presented by the employees of the four fox hunts with which the earl was closely associated (Wentworth, Cantley, Yacht and Grove); and a third, an antique porringer, by the parishioners of Wentworth. A fourth silver bowl, presented by the miners of Elsecar Main and Low Stubbin collieries, was used at the christening itself.

The 7,000 official guests dined in the riding school in the stable block (where 1,000 were accommodated) and in six enormous marquees which had taken 100 men to erect. The caterers, Lyons of London, were put in charge of feeding the 7,000 official guests, and 300 waiters were dispatched from London by special train. The general public were given the opportunity to buy beef sandwiches, the beef being cut from a roasted ox.

The entertainment for the general public included local bands and roundabouts. Then at a quarter to six in the evening, when it was quite dark, the family, the invited guests and the general public were entertained by a magnificent firework display. Managed by the famous firm of Brocks, it was reputed to be the biggest private display for five years. The set pieces included portraits of the earl and countess with the motto 'Long life to the Heir'; Niagara Falls rolling its waters down 'in limpid fire'; and in a realistic prelude of what was to become a reality within a few years, a British 'dreadnought' battleship attacked and beat what the *Rotherham Advertiser* called 'the Dreadnought of a "Continental Power"'.

Viscount Milton became the eighth earl Fitzwilliam in 1943, but was killed in a light aircraft accident in 1948.

'Christians are Handier than Horses'

Children in Coalmines in the Nineteenth Century

One of the most revealing documents published in the Victorian period is the report relating to the Children's Employment Commission of the early 1840s enquiring into the employment of children in mines. The sub-commissioner responsible for collecting evidence and writing up the report on the employment of children in mines in the South Yorkshire area was Jelinger C Symons Esq. His report on children in mines in West and South Yorkshire, which is dated July 1841, covers 42 pages with 17 pages of appendices followed by 73 pages of depositions from 299 separate witnesses gathered in early 1841. Symons interviewed mine owners, managers, miners, the children who worked in the pits, and a variety of other witnesses including doctors and clergymen. He investigated practices and conditions in collieries and ironstone pits, large and small.

The reformers who pressed for this commission to take place were concerned about the physical and spiritual welfare of the children. Others saw the child labour force as a necessary evil, and it was condoned not only by capitalists large and small but also by parents, the latter seeing children from a very young age not as dependants but as important components of the family economic unit. The underground steward at a coal pit near Thorpe Hesley told Symons that 'it would do great harm to a man who has a large family to prevent a lad from opening a [trap] door or being in a pit till he is 11 years old.' One divisive issue even among those who condoned child labour was the employment of girls underground and, as we shall see, Symons witnessed girl miners on many occasions in South Yorkshire, although two of the biggest employers — Earl Fitzwilliam and Newton Chambers at Thorncliffe — did not allow this form of labour.

Many of Symons's main witnesses were the children themselves. Some of the children interviewed were painfully honest; others may have been 'briefed'. The same must be true of the adult witnesses who would not have wanted to be dismissed for showing their employer in a poor light. However, even with these reservations in mind, what comes across is a graphic portrayal of heavy, debilitating work, often in atrocious conditions, usually in semi-darkness and with the strong possibility of physical injury. Symons described graphically what it must have been like for young children being introduced to a pit for the first time:

The springs which ooze through the best cased shafts, trickle down its sides, and keep up a perpetual drizzle below. The chamber or area at the bottom of the shaft is almost always sloppy and muddy, and the escape from it consists of a labyrinth of black passages, often not above four feet square …

Many must have been afraid, and would have faced every day's work with fear and loathing. During their childhood they might have first-hand experience of accidents caused by explosions of fire-damp, suffocation from black-damp, roof falls, breaking of ropes and chains in the shaft, inundations of water and blows from runaway coal wagons.

Children were employed underground in three main ways: as trappers, horse-drivers and hurriers. In a deep pit, ventilation air was drawn down a 'downcast' shaft, then circulated through the workings and ascended an 'upcast' shaft (in this period,

Memorial in the churchyard at Silkstone to the twenty-six children and young adults killed in a flood at Huskar pit in 1838. The victims included eleven females aged from eight to seventeen, and fifteen males aged from seven to sixteen.

often the same one that coal was wound up, and up and down which the miners were carried from and to their work). In order that the fresh air made no short cuts, trapdoors were placed along the main underground roadway (main gate). The responsibility for making sure that the trap doors were always closed between the passage of full or empty coal wagons (called corves) was with the trappers, and this role was entrusted to the youngest children in a pit — they were not yet big or strong enough to do other jobs. Symons described it thus:

> *Their duty consists in sitting in a little hole, scooped out for them in the side of the gates behind each door, where they sit with a string in their hands attached to the door, and pull it open the moment they hear the corves at hand, and the moment it has passed they let the door fall too* [sic], *which it does of its own weight ... They have nothing else to do; but, as their office must be performed from the repassing of the first to the passing of the last corve during the day, they are in the pit the whole time it is worked, frequently above twelve hours a day. They sit, moreover in the dark ...*

He went on to say that 'Trappers are on the whole, more cheerful than might be expected; and it is not unusual to hear them singing as they sit in their holes.' Samuel Hirst, a nine year old trapper at Earl Fitzwilliam's pit at Jump, was questioned by Symons. He said he sat by himself and did not have a light. He said he sat still all day and never did anything except open and shut the door. He said he'd rather be at school than down the pit. He said that 'it's only sometimes that they pay [beat] me'. When Symons interviewed another trapper, George Lindley at Gawber pit, who was nine and had been trapping for three years, the boy told him that when his light went out 'I smoke my pipe. I smoke a quarten of tobacco every week.' At the same pit he encountered Sarah Gooder, an eight year old trapper. She told Symons that she trapped without a light and was scared.

The best occupation for children, according to Symons, was that of horse-driver. Horses were used to take corves to the pit bottom in large collieries where the main gate was long and the coal seams sufficiently thick to allow the use of animals. Horse-drivers were involved in little heavy work, only being called upon to exert their

A young trapper (right) at work.

A hurrier, from the *Children's Employment Commission Report, 1842*

strength if a corf accidentally came off the rails on which it was travelling. The horses were well trained, and the drivers sat in the front corf (they were usually in trains of six to eight) when taking empties back to the coal face. At Earl Fitzwilliam's pits at Elsecar and Jump, each horse-driver had an assistant. There were twenty-one horse-drivers and their assistants employed there.

By far the most common form of employment of children underground was that of hurrier or trammer. Hurriers were employed to convey coal in corves from the coal face to the pit bottom or, where horses were used, from the coal face to the main gate. Unlike the trappers and horse-drivers, the hurriers were employed directly by the miners (getters). During a day's work the hurriers pushed their corves considerable distances. At Mr Clarke's collieries at Silkstone, Symons calculated that, on average, the hurriers had to push a loaded corf, weighing eight hundredweight (400kg), 150 yards (135m) from the coal faces to the horse gate and back again twenty times during a shift — a distance of three and a half miles (5.5km). At Traviss and Horsfall's pit at Worsbrough, the distances worked were considerably longer: hurriers had to convey their corves 400 yards (365m) full and 400 yards empty twenty times during a day's work — an overall distance of more than nine miles (14.5km).

At Messrs Thorpe's pits at Gawber, Symons likened the work of two sisters he saw hurrying there to slavery: 'I have no hesitation in adding that were they galley slaves their work could not be more oppressive, and I believe would not in all probability be so much so.' And yet Mr J C Sutcliffe, the general agent for the pit, while admitting that the corves in the pit were heavier than in other local pits (12½ cwt/635kg when full), was of the opinion that 'a girl of sixteen can hurry one of these corves very well and do her day's work with ease.' This evidence contrasts markedly with that given by Ann Eggley at the same pit:

> The work is far too hard for me; the sweat runs off me all over sometimes. I'm very tired at night. Sometimes when we get home at night we have not power to wash us, and then we go to bed. Sometimes we fall asleep in the chair. Father said last night it was both a shame and a disgrace to work as we do, but there was nought else for us to do.

Where the gates were steep, great strength was needed either to hold the full corf back or to push the empty corf uphill back to the face. Symons said it was not uncommon to see bald hurriers 'owing to pushing corves up steep board-gates with their heads'. In thin-seam pits there were often no rails and the roofs were so low that the corves had to be pulled like sledges on chains fastened round the hurriers' waists by belts.

In South Yorkshire, Symons said, trappers earned generally sixpence (2½p) per day. The hurriers, in the thick coal pits, earned about five shillings (25p) a week at eleven; those of fourteen to seventeen were paid eight shillings (40p) . Miners' earnings varied according to their strength and industry. Young able-bodied getters in thick coal pits earned twenty or twenty-five shillings (£1 or £1.25p) a week. In the thin coal pits, wages were ten or twenty per cent less.

The age at which children are reported to have started work almost beggars belief. According to Symons, 'there were well-attested instances of children being taken into coal-pits as early as five years of age…'. Edward Ellis Esq, a Silkstone surgeon, said that he had twenty-five years' professional experience among colliers and he was of the opinion that children went into pits at the age of five very frequently. The Rev Richard Morton, curate of Dodworth, said that parents got their children into the pits 'as soon as they think they can do anything', adding 'I have been told that some have gone by the time they have been five years old'. Symons thought such cases were rare but that many did begin work at seven. He reckoned eight was the normal age for beginning work underground.

Symons reported that in thin-seam pits there was a temptation to bring in young children simply because they were small and could cope better with the low roofs. One Sheffield coal manager actually said in his evidence that 'Christians are handier than horses …'.

On average miners, including the children, worked between ten and eleven hours a day six days a week. Each day each team of miners — and the children were key members of these teams — 'got' a certain quota of coal or ironstone. Towards the end of a week or fortnight, depending on when they got paid, longer hours were frequently worked to make up for any lost time.

Work usually commenced between five and six in the morning, and work began as soon as the coal face was reached; this was almost immediately in a small pit, but could

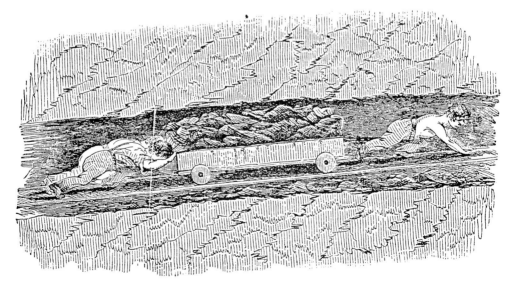

Hurriers in a thin-seam pit, from the *Children's Employment Commission Report, 1842*.

take up to an hour in an extensive deep colliery where the miners had to wait to take the cage to the pit bottom and then walk to their work place. A collier at Messrs Day and Twibell's pit in Barnsley told Symons that young children were 'taken out of their beds at four o'clock, and between that and five, throughout the year'. The miners usually left the pits between three and five in the afternoon. Night work was unusual.

It is clear from the evidence that Symons collected that the children often began their work without having any breakfast, often took meagre rations to work, and were often too tired to eat when they got home. When he interviewed Elizabeth Day, a seventeen year old hurrier at Hopwoods pit in Barnsley, she said she had bread and a bit of fat [dripping] for her dinner in the pit; some of the hurriers also had 'a sup of beer'; she said she drank the water that ran through the pit. One collier told Symons that hurrying was 'very slavish work', yet he had known boys work twelve hours without more than 'a bit of dry bread to eat'. A Mr Crooks, a Barnsley surgeon, in a letter written to Symons, said that on his rounds that day he had ridden by a group of miners' cottages, and a neighbouring farmer had told him that many of the children there worked underground and that many 'who had thoughtless parents' were badly fed. He said some of them were sent to work without breakfast, took little to eat with them and had 'but coarse fare when they returned'. In contrast, when interviewed by Symons, Mr Crooks said that he had heard that 'there is enough bread lying about in a pit to feed a pig, and when they come out they have hot dinners generally'.

Symons was of the view that the vices of the children of colliers were much less than those of 'the manufacturing class'. He put this down to the fact that they were 'much more closely confined and tired when their work is done', and because they did not work together for long periods. Having said that, he believed that their ignorance was just as great as the children who worked in factories, if not more so. He also reported that there was a 'fearful amount' of swearing and indecent language in the pits.

There was general concern about the lack of education among the mining population. They were at work during the day, and too tired or wished to take advantage of sunshine and fresh air at the weekends. The opinion of William Newbould, a coal master, seems quite out of touch: 'They could learn in the evenings if they chose; they are not too tired with their work to do so.' Timothy Marshall's view (he was a miner at Darton) seems more realistic: 'they are both tired and disinclined to learn when they have done work'.

Symons had much to say and report about the employment of girls underground. Girls, he said, performed all the various mining jobs — trapping, hurrying, filling, riddling, tipping and occasionally getting. He went on to say that one of the most disgusting sights he had ever seen, at the day pits at Hunshelf Bank near Penistone, was that of 'young females, dressed like boys in trousers, crawling on all fours, with belts round their waists and chains passing between their legs'. He said the gate in the pit was not more than a yard (90cm) high, and in some places not much more than two feet (60cm).

At Messrs Charlesworth's pit at Silkstone, Symons interviewed Ann Fern, a hurrier, who had been working there for five years. She seemed resigned to her fate. She said she was up at half past four, went down the pit at five, and got out at four or five in the

A girl hurrier (left), from the *Children's Employment Commission Report, 1842*.

afternoon. She said she liked the pit but would rather be in service, 'but had never tried'. She said it was hard work but 'should be worked hard anywhere I daresay'. She had had a broken leg while working as a trapper when she was younger.

The sub-commissioner was also concerned about the degree of nakedness among the girls, and the effect this had on the girls themselves and miners with whom they worked:

> *In great numbers of the coal-pits in this district the men work in a state of perfect nakedness, and are in this state assisted in their labour by females of all ages, from girls of six years old to women of twenty-one, these females being themselves quite naked down to the waist.*

He also had something to say about what he called 'bastardy' in the pits, going on to record the fact that the character of the miners in general was such that it was the general practice to marry the girls they had seduced.

Symons concluded that the mining children were growing up in what he variously called 'a state of Heathen ignorance' or 'a state of absolute and appalling ignorance'. Because they started work at an early age, were out of sight during the day and took advantage of the fresh air and light on Sundays, the mining population lived, he said, 'out of sight of the rest of the community, and almost wholly out of its ken: they are reached by none of our institutions'.

Mr George Traviss, a Barnsley coal owner, told Symons that he did not think children were overworked so as to hurt them. 'They always appear to me', said Traviss, 'to be very cheerful, and run about and play when they come out of the pit in the evening'. The same sentiments were also expressed by other coal owners and managers. Symons's riposte in his report was typically direct and neatly sums up the

Children being lowered down a small coal-pit.

situation of the many children working underground in pits in South Yorkshire at the beginning of the Victorian period:

> *The evidence given by some witnesses, that the children are cheerful when they get out of the pit, is somewhat akin to evidence that people are cheerful when they get out of prison.*

To the twenty-first century reader, Symons's report contains compelling evidence of the wrongness of committing children to work underground from a very early age: it was likely to have a severe impact on their physical health, their morals and their education, let alone the psychological damage that was done. The practice seems to us callous and depraved. And yet it was not thought to be wicked by coal owners and many of the parents of the children involved. The coal owners had a vested interest in getting out of the pits the largest amount of coal for the least cost, and the parents saw their children, when they had reached a certain age, as contributors to the family's income rather than as dependants. It needs to be remembered that there was no compulsory education system, no old age pensions, and trade unions were in their infancy.

The outcome of the enquiry was that when the report was laid before parliament in 1842, a bill was brought forward by Lord Ashley (later the earl of Shaftesbury) and an act of Parliament was passed on the 4th August of that year forbidding the employment of girls and women underground, and making unlawful the employment of boys in pits under the age of ten.

Blacklegs, Bludgeons and Broken Heads

The Thorncliffe Collieries Dispute, 1869–70

Taking a country walk through the wooded Thorncliffe Valley and in and around the former Tankersley deer park (now largely converted to a golf course), about halfway between Barnsley and Sheffield, it is difficult to believe that you are in the vicinity of one of the most celebrated labour disputes of the nineteenth century. This was a dispute that rivalled, in its physical confrontations between locked-out miners and the forces of law and order, the more recent national miners' strike of 1984. After the dispute was over, the employer, Newton Chambers & Co, described it as 'the most determined contest between capital and labour which is to be found in the mining history of this or any other country'. They went on to say that the action of the miners created 'not only indignation but astonishment in this and other countries'.

The dispute took place between March 1869 and August 1870, and during this eighteen month period some 850 miners were in dispute with their employer. The dispute stemmed from the decision by Newton Chambers to reduce wages by seven and a half per cent and their refusal to negotiate with the Miners' Union. The miners were required to work an eight hour day when required to do so, always negotiate individually over wages, and compulsorily pay subscriptions to the company's Accident Club. And this decision was taking place only three years after a nine month lock-out over wages and conditions in 1866 when Newton Chambers had refused to accept the terms conceded at other local collieries.

The sources for the study of the dispute and the violent activity associated with it are unusually rich and varied. They include the records of the Miners' Union, Newton Chambers company records, newspaper reports, articles in the *Mining Journal*, letters to local and national newspapers, reports of court proceedings, recruitment posters for non-union labour and two personal diaries.

The evidence reveals a situation in which there was constant tension, anxiety, plotting and counter-plotting, and a general air of foreboding. The employer stood firm and attempted to replace the locked-out miners with 'blackleg' labour from other coalfields, mainly from Northumberland, Durham, Derbyshire and Staffordshire. The unemployed miners, not surprisingly, tried to persuade the blacklegs to return home. They succeeded in this to some extent, but inevitably the trickle of blackleg labour increased and this was combatted by outbreaks of violent behaviour aimed at intimidating the newcomers. The lives of senior members of the firm were also threatened. This, in turn, led to police and military reinforcements being brought to

Cottages in the former Tankersley Park.

the area, and inevitably the tension and antagonism increased still further. Thorncliffe and the neighbouring industrial communities in Chapeltown and High Green must have sometimes seemed to be under siege.

William Nesbitt, foreman engineer with Newton Chambers, who had come to work for the firm in January 1869, and who kept a regular and detailed diary during his first six years there, noted the beginning of the dispute in a very matter-of-fact way, not knowing how long and severe it would be (spelling in the diary extracts has been standardised):

Wednesday 24th [March]
Finished 3 foot Pulley for hay cutting machine for the Company's farm, being five days in the lathe.
Mr Thomas Chamber's youngest daughter was married today to Mr Hawett of Nottingham and the affair came off very quietly.
All the coalminers of the Thorncliffe Coal Company came out on strike.

By the beginning of April he noted that several policemen had arrived at Thorncliffe 'to protect property and the men that have started work at the pits, against the men that are out on strike'. The next day (2nd April) he noted that two blacklegs who had started work at Thorncliffe drift pit were 'guarded to work by policemen'. A month into the strike and with no sign of a settlement, Nesbitt noted that orders had been given 'for all the tenants to clear out of Thorncliffe Cottages as he [Mr John Chambers, the partner principally concerned with the collieries] wanted the houses for his blacksheep'. Despite the fact that some newcomers were being induced to return home before taking up residence and work at Thorncliffe (Nesbitt recorded blacklegs being met at Chapeltown railway station on the 27th April and having their return journeys paid for them), the eviction of the locked-out miners and their families from the Thorncliffe Rows and the installation in their place of blackleg families led to the first major outbreak of violent behaviour.

Nesbitt was living on the Thorncliffe Rows at the time and had a close-up view of the event:

> *April 29th*
> *Last night at 10 o'clock the miners attacked the blacksheep in Thorncliffe Cottages in a body. Drove the policemen out and broke all the glass windows in five houses, but no-one was injured. They were about two hundred in number. The policemen ran in all directions, some hiding themselves in the water closets.*

Subsequently twenty-two of the locked-out miners received summonses to court for riotous behaviour, and the ringleaders were sent to prison for a month.

Throughout the rest of 1869 as the dispute continued, there were outbreaks of violence of varying degrees of severity and periods of mounting tension when it was believed a major outbreak was about to occur, these being accompanied by reports of 'many strangers' being in the district. Arriving blacklegs continued to be met at local railway stations by angry crowds.

As the conflict raged, John Chambers died, and for a moment the dispute was forgotten as the local community mourned one of its leading members. William Nesbitt noted in his diary for the 11th June that:

> [At] *10.30 am* [A] *large number of miners and the workmen of Thorncliffe Iron Works, mustered at the residence of the late Mr J Chambers to pay their last respects to their departed friend, which will be interred at Tankersley Church Yard at 12.30pm. On the procession leaving Chapeltown it would muster about four hundred people besides 12 carriages.*

George Dawson, manager of the ironworks and, as we shall see, a man believed by the locked-out miners to be a major obstacle to a quick settlement in their favour, specifically referred to their good behaviour in his diary entry on the day of the funeral: 'Mr John Chambers buried at Tankersley. The colliers on strike followed the procession and behaved well.'

But a settlement to the dispute was still far away and, as the year wore on, positions became entrenched, tensions became almost unbearable and violence was increasingly expected.

William Nesbitt recorded in his diary on 21st October that at 6 pm the alarm whistle had started to blow at Tankersley Colliery. He went on:

> *About 100 miners made their appearance in the neighbourhood armed with sticks in a threatening attitude, but all passed off quietly. Three troops of policemen were brought from Sheffield for a wild goose chase.*

By the 23rd October it was reported in the *Sheffield and Rotherham Independent* that representatives of Newton Chambers were seeking the assistance of the army in the

The attack on Tankersley Colliery on the 7th January 1870, as illustrated in *The Graphic*.

form of a permanent garrison because the neighbourhood was 'in a state of constant terror' and an attack was expected on the homes of the working miners. In November 1869 the union admitted that as many as 100 blacksheep were working in the collieries, and in the face of what must have been a steady stream of new recruits, as winter approached and then set in, large-scale violence erupted again in order to intimidate the blackleg miners. On the 7th January 1870 a crowd attacked Tankersley pit and broke windows, smashed lamps and pushed several corves (coal wagons) down the shaft. William Vernon, the engine minder at Tankersley pit, alerted the local population and the police in Barnsley by a long and continuous blowing of the pit buzzer, and as the rioters broke into the engine house he hid himself under the floorboards to escape recriminations. William Nesbitt recorded in his diary that they searched for Vernon 'to take his life'. As the attackers dispersed at a run into the woods and across Tankersley Park when confronted by police, one miner fell down a quarry and broke both his legs.

The senior partners of Newton Chambers were also worried because of threats on their lives. George Dawson noted in his diary that on the 11th December he had been warned that the colliers contemplated doing him an injury 'in consequence of their belief that the dispute would be settled if I was not in the way'. On the 20th December he noted that 'we had a dreadful threatening letter at Thorncliffe this morning. I do not know what the end of it will be.'

By January 1870 matters were coming to a head. An attack took place on Tankersley Colliery on the 7th January as noted above, and on the 10th January George Dawson recorded in his diary that:

> *Today we have been advised to be never out after dark as the unionists intend to try the effect of powder and shot. I trust to the loving hand of Providence to deliver me from their cruel assassination, but it is very miserable to think that at any hour my dear children may be fatherless.*

William Vernon in old age with his wife Elizabeth. Besides alerting the local population and the Barnsley police to the riotous attack on Tankersley Colliery, William Vernon also goes down in local history for starting the first Co-operative Store (a branch of the famous Barnsley British Co-operative Society) in the Chapeltown district from the front room of his cottage on Warren Lane.

Threatening letters also continued to be received by leading members of the company. One addressed to Arthur Marshall Chambers in early 1870 went as follows:

> *Mr Chambers Sir. Prepare to meet thy God, as I insist on thee been a dead man before long if thou means to keep us this winter. We are determined not to let you see the end of it if thou means to let us clam [ie starve] & starve. We mean to have it out of you you bugger as thy Days are numbered. So prepare to meet thy God.*
>
> *yours truly one who wishes you in hell fire.*

Then on Friday the 21st January at seven o'clock in the morning, a crowd of men variously estimated at between 300 and 1,500, some 'armed with pistols, some with bludgeons, the heads of which bristled with spikes, some with picks' according to the *Sheffield and Rotherham Independent*, simultaneously attacked the backs and fronts of the cottages in the Westwood Rows. These cottages had been built specifically to house blackleg miners and their families in a relatively remote spot on the edge of the woods between the Thorncliffe Ironworks and Tankersley Colliery. Their remoteness gave rise to the local name of 'Newfoundland'. The cottages were defended on the morning of the attack by a force of ten policemen who were overwhelmed, though not before they had despatched a messenger to Barnsley for reinforcements. In the ensuing mayhem, windows were smashed, doors and furniture demolished, houses looted and an unsuccessful attempt made to set fire to the houses by burning clothing, bedclothes and broken furniture.

While this was happening, the police reinforcements from Barnsley arrived on the scene and reportedly set about the crowd with cutlasses to which the miners replied with their bludgeons. No one was killed, though at least one policemen and one miner received serious injuries.

Police reinforcements dispersing the rioters at Westwood Rows on the 21st January 1870, as portrayed in *The Graphic*.

William Nesbitt recorded the riot in graphic detail in his diary:

> At 7am the alarm was given that the union miners locked out of the Thorncliffe Collieries
> had commenced an attack on the houses of the Black or non-unionist miners at work in
> the pits, and in a few minutes it proved to be correct, as the shouts or yells of the mob
> were heard for a mile distant from the scene of action. The mob numbered about 1,000 men
> and the destruction of property amounted to about £400. Every door and window in 30
> houses were broken to pieces besides both men and women and children most brutally
> treated by the lawless mob. The police attacked them in different quarters but being
> overpowered by numbers they were obliged to retreat for a time. They again advanced with
> drawn cutlass, and beat them off, but not before several were wounded, and one taken
> prisoner.
>
> On examining the houses at Westwood, it was found that all the furniture, bedding,
> clothing and other valuables in the houses were burned by fire or otherwise destroyed.
> Many of the inmates were left without any clothes, other than those they had been sleeping
> with during the night. The last attack was on the Tankersley Pit, but the police succeeded
> in driving them off before damage was done.
>
> 8pm. All quiet, Police reinforced to 100 men.

On the day following the riot, Saturday the 22nd January, there was still an air of
tension in the area, but things became quieter with the arrival in the late afternoon
from Sheffield Barracks of fifty-four men and three officers of the 22nd Regiment.
Then the next day, Sunday, when most people were not at work, crowds came from far
and wide to visit the scene of the riot, and William Nesbitt recorded the event in some
detail:

> Great numbers of people arrived by each train from Sheffield and Barnsley during the
> morning, and the roads were thronged from all quarters, by people enquiring their way to
> Westwood Row, the scene of the riot. At noon more than 2,000 people were in the district,
> some to examine the wreck, and others to do as much mischief as possible. Several
> encounters took place when they had a chance of a blacksheep. Two or three heads were
> broken, and one grinder from Sheffield taken prisoner. Many shots were fired from both
> parties during the day and much threatening language on both sides.

A week after the riot, twenty-five of the rioters were brought before the magistrates at
Barnsley and this induced another disturbance. William Nesbitt again recorded the
details in his diary:

> January 28th
> The Thorncliffe rioters were brought before the magistrates at Barnsley and remanded to
> Wakefield for a week. Four were set at liberty … On removing the prisoners to the railway
> station they were guarded by the police, and 50 of the 22 Regiment to keep order. All were
> safely removed but as the witnesses were leaving for their homes, they were stoned by the
> mob and several of the soldiers were hit with stones, and one woman had her head cut with
> a stone, the famous Nellie of Westwood Row.

Twenty-three men were eventually sent for trial at York assizes, eleven receiving
sentences of imprisonment, three of them for five years.

The Westwood Rows in the late 1960s shortly before their demolition.

Following the January disturbances, soldiers, about 100 in all, were quartered for six months at the workman's hall at Mortomley Lane End and at Tankersley Farm. An uneasy peace returned to the area, accompanied by attempts by a number of prominent local men, most notably the earl of Wharncliffe and Mr W S Stanhope, to bring about a resolution to the crisis. Throughout the lock-out, Newton Chambers refused to negotiate with John Normansell, the local miners' leader, referring to organised labour as 'the tyranny of numbers'.

The dispute lasted another seven months, ending on the 17 August 1870. Men were taken on at reduced wages, former workmen had to apply for re-employment on an individual basis (known or suspected troublemakers not being taken on again) and there were no vacancies at Thorncliffe drift pit, presumably because all the places were already filled by blacklegs, local and migrant. The concessions made by the employers were relatively minor: subscriptions to the Accident Club were to be optional rather than compulsory; all Saturday working was reduced to a half day (it had previously been one Saturday per fortnight); and although fortnightly pay days remained, money could be advanced on a weekly basis if earned.

A Remarkable Literary and Artistic Family
The Gattys of Ecclesfield

A visitor to Ecclesfield vicarage in 1866, who did not know anything of the family living there, could be excused for thinking that he or she had stumbled on a writers' and artists' colony. The mother might have been observed editing contributions to a new children's magazine, of which she was editor. The father might have been seen writing what he called a 'supplemental' chapter to a new edition of Joseph Hunter's *History of Hallamshire*. Their second eldest daughter, Juliana, still in her mid-twenties, may have been in her room writing the latest instalment of *Mrs Overtheway's Remembrances* to be published in her mother's magazine in the following year. Another couple of daughters might have been seen checking proofs for the mother. The eldest daughter Margaret might have been seen working on a final version of a watercolour painting of 'Old Mother Shaw' the mother of the village constable; and son Alfred, just twenty, might have been heard putting the final touches to the words and music of his children's song 'Going to School' which was published in 1867.

But these were not full-time writers, artists or composers but the vicar of an enormous parish, a vicar's wife, daughters who in practical terms were unpaid curates and who carried out a diversity of parish tasks on behalf of their father, and a son who was destined for an outstanding career as a genealogist at the College of Arms.

The Gatty parents came to Ecclesfield in September 1839. Alfred Gatty, with his new wife Margaret (they were married on the 8th July 1839), had come to a very large parish covering 50,000 acres or nearly seventy-eight square miles (200km²). Gatty was succeeding his bride's uncle.

Alfred Gatty was born in London in 1813, the son of a solicitor, and educated at Charterhouse, Eton and Oxford. He was to remain vicar of Ecclesfield until his death in 1903 at the age of eighty-nine. He became a doctor of divinity and sub-dean of York. He recorded details of his long incumbency at Ecclesfield in his *A Life at One Living* (1884). He also wrote collections of sermons for 'country congregations and family reading' which were sold at railway station bookstalls throughout the country. But he is best known locally as the reviser and editor of the definitive editions (1869 and 1875) of Joseph Hunter's *History of Hallamshire* (first published in 1819) and for *Sheffield: Past and Present* (1873), the first attempt at 'a clear and continuous history' of the then town.

Margaret Gatty (1809–73) was the daughter of the Rev Alexander John Scott, Lord Nelson's chaplain at Trafalgar, and later vicar at Southminster in Essex and Catterick in the North Riding. Mrs Gatty was multi-talented and had a much wider literary

The chess players: Alfred and Margaret Gatty shortly after their marriage in 1839.

reputation than her husband. She was a writer for children, in which capacity she had a world-wide reputation and readership. She is best known for her *Parables from Nature* and her editorship of *Aunt Judy's Magazine* from 1866 until her death in 1873 (after which it was edited by her third-eldest daughter Horatia, with assistance for two years from Juliana, her second-eldest daughter, of whom much more below). She was compared in her lifetime to Hans Christian Andersen. Mrs Gatty's editorship of *Aunt Judy's Magazine* resulted in the provision of endowed sickbeds in the Hospital for Sick Children in Great Ormond Street, London. Her readers from all over the country and from all over the world were invited to contribute whatever they could to the sponsorship of cots. Even family pets were recorded as sending subscriptions. By 1876 a girls' cot and a boys' cot had been permanently endowed, the first in any London hospital. Readers in India endowed a bed called 'Simla' and there was even one endowed by readers in St Petersburg, Russia.

Mrs Gatty was also a very talented landscape artist, as her illustrations in early editions of *Parables from Nature* and her unpublished watercolours affirm. Some of her etchings are in the British Museum. She was also an expert on sundials, and published *The Book of Sun-Dials* in 1873; she is still revered by members of the British Sundial Society. She was also an outstanding marine biologist, a seemingly odd distinction for someone who spent most of her adult life as far as it is possible to be from the English seaside. It seems that she went to Hastings during the winter of 1848–9 to recuperate from illness following the birth of her seventh child Undine, and a local doctor

Aunt Judy's Magazine cot at the Great Ormond Street Hospital for Sick Children.

suggested she might take up the hobby of seaweed collection to keep her active and aid her recovery. The hobby became an obsession, and her children made fun of her preoccupation with seaweed collecting on family holidays. A poem by daughter Juliana, a pastiche of Kingsley's *The Sands of Dee*, begins:

> O Gatty's! go and call your mother home
> Call your mother home
> At least in time for tea!
> The breakfast, lunch, and dinner go and come
> Unheeded, at the sea.

The hobby culminated in 1863 with the publication of the two-volume *British Sea-Weeds* with eighty colour plates containing 384 figures. The introduction includes a detailed dress guide for female seaweed collectors, including reference to the problem of petticoats — 'those necessary draperies'. An Australian seaweed *Gattya pinella* and a marine worm *Gattia spectabilis* are named after Mrs Gatty. Her seaweed collection is in Sheffield City Museum and has recently been described by Derek Whiteley, the museum's former keeper of natural history, as 'of international importance'.

Dr and Mrs Gatty had ten children, but two died in infancy. The surviving four sons and four daughters were of rare talent. Two of the Gatty sons were knighted: Alfred Scott Gatty (1847–1918), the second son, who became Sir Alfred Scott-Gatty instead of plain Gatty, rose to become garter king of arms at the College of Arms and was in charge of the organisation of King Edward VII's lying in state and funeral, and King George V's coronation. He was also an authority on patent medicines and an accomplished composer, writing the words and music for a large number of children's songs and Christmas carols — many first published in *Aunt Judy's Magazine* — and also 'plantation ballads', of which one authority claimed he was the inventor. He certainly popularised this type of song in this country, and it is said he and his wife were star performers at fashionable charity events in late Victorian and Edwardian London. He was nicknamed 'the minstrel boy' by a cartoonist in *Vanity Fair* magazine. The third surviving son, Sir Stephen Herbert Gatty (1849–1922), was a colonial high court judge, becoming chief justice of Gibraltar. Stephen's daughter Hester married the poet Siegfried Sassoon.

Charles Tindal Gatty (1851–1928), the youngest son, was at various times a museum curator, private secretary, biographer and journalist. He was a friend of John Ruskin. Reginald Alfred Gatty (1844–1914), the eldest son, went into the Church, and was rector of Bradfield and then rector of Hooton Roberts. He had a wide range of talents and interests. He amassed an important collection of local sixteenth- and seventeenth-century oak furniture, and was an enthusiastic and pioneering field archaeologist — parts of his collection of prehistoric stone and flint tools are in Rotherham's Clifton Park Museum and Sheffield City Museum. He was also an author of songs, writing the words to children's songs and carols written by his brother Alfred (two of the carols still being part of the repertoire of singers of local carols in South Yorkshire). Ralph Vaughan Williams was a visitor to the vicarage at Hooton Roberts, and the local tradition is that 'On Linden Lea' was composed on one of his visits there. Reginald's son Nicholas was a composer of orchestral pieces, chamber music and operas.

Sir Alfred Scott-Gatty in his court uniform.

'Julie [Juliana] and Dot [Horatia] — The Harvest Field 1865',
a watercolour by their sister Madge (Margaret).

Margaret Scott Gatty (1840–1900), the eldest daughter, undertook editorial duties for her mother until her marriage in 1868, and was an accomplished watercolourist and illustrator. She illustrated the first edition of her sister Juliana's début book *Melchior's Dream and Other Tales*, and two of her drawings appear in the third edition of her mother's *Parables from Nature* (1861). Her literary and artistic assistance were both terminated from 1868 when she married Francis Patrick Smith, eldest son of William Smith of Barnes Hall, and became the mother of nine boys during the following fifteen years (see pages 115-122).

Horatia Katharine Frances (1846–1945), the third daughter, always known as 'Dot', was a critically active member of the Gatty literary and scientific enterprise at Ecclesfield Vicarage. She closely assisted her mother in the collection and classification of seaweeds, kept the specimen collection intact after her mother's death and eventually passed it to Sheffield City Museum. She also revised Mrs Gatty's *Book of Sun-Dials* with family friend Eleanor Lloyd. She also worked closely with her mother on the editorship of *Aunt Judy's Magazine*, especially as Margaret Gatty's paralytic illness became more and more severe, and after her mother's death in 1873 she edited it jointly with Juliana for two years and then on her own until its demise in 1885. In that year Juliana died, and Horatia wrote *Juliana Horatia Ewing and Her Books*, which was later re-issued with a selection of Juliana's letters. Horatia married Thomas Eden and for a number of years they ran a preparatory school near Rugby. She lived until 1945 when she was within two months of her hundredth birthday, by which time both her mother's and her sister Juliana's literary works were out of copyright.

The role played by the youngest daughter, Undine Marcia (born 1848), is much less clear than those of the other Gatty siblings. She did not marry until 1884 and as the last of the children to live at home, and to continue to provide domestic and parochial help to her ageing father, her imminent marriage to the Rev W Ward and emigration to Australia was a great blow to Alfred, who is reputed to have said that he would give up his intended second marriage if she would give up hers. It was to be Undine's daughter, Chrisabel Maxwell, who would write the full-length biography of Margaret Gatty and her daughter Juliana (*Mrs Gatty and Mrs Ewing*, Constable, 1949).

It was Alfred and Margaret Gatty's second daughter, Juliana Horatia (1841–85), who gained the most renown. She had an even greater literary reputation as a children's writer than her mother. She wrote more than 100 children's stories, most of them first published in her mother's magazine. She was always a delicate child but from an early age took charge of activities in the nursery, being the chief storyteller, and organiser of games and play-acting. She was the 'Aunt Judy' of her mother's books *Aunt Judy's Tales* (1859), *Aunt Judy's Letters* (1862) and of course of *Aunt Judy's Magazine*. Juliana published her first story in 1861 at the age of nineteen.

In 1867 she married Captain (later Major and eventually Colonel) Alexander Ewing. Within days of their marriage they took ship to Canada, where Captain Ewing was stationed for two years at Fredericton, New Brunswick. In late 1869 they returned to England, where they stayed till 1879. The now Major Ewing was then posted to Malta and then to Ceylon but Juliana was too unwell to accompany him. She got as far as Paris but then had to be accompanied home. From 1883 until her death in 1885 at the age of only forty-three, the couple were stationed near Taunton in Somerset. She

Juliana and Alexander Ewing and their dog Hector, in Fredericton, New Brunswick.

is buried in the churchyard at Trull near Taunton, where there is a window in the church dedicated to herself and her husband.

In her lifetime, Juliana Ewing was compared to Lewis Carroll and Robert Louis Stevenson, was much admired by John Ruskin, and her books were printed by the tens of thousands. Baden Powell took the name 'Brownies' for the junior branch of the Girl Guides from the characters in one of her stories. Perhaps her best known story is *Jackanapes*, the tale of the village boy who became a soldier and who died saving his village friend. It was famously illustrated by Randolph Caldecott. Arnold Bennett said it was a story 'which must have been told a thousand times, but never better'.

Juliana loved her local patch in south-west Yorkshire: the church, the vicarage and its grounds, the local countryside and the local people. It not only fed her literary imagination throughout her life, it sustained her in illness, like her mother and sisters she drew and painted it, and time and again on the army postings with her husband in different parts of Britain and in Canada it manifested itself in bouts of homesickness.

The remarkable thing about the countryside that inspired so much of Juliana's writing is its small compass — it was about two miles (3km) in extent from east to west and about a mile (1.5km) from north to south. It contained for her both a set of of general well-loved memories — fields, hedges, stone walls, trees, woods, streams, mossy banks, flowers, grasses and ferns, sandstone cottages, bridges and paths — and real places like Lee Shroggs Wood, Greno Wood, St Mary's Church at Ecclesfield, the vicarage and its gardens, the Whitley Valley, and the villages of Ecclesfield and Grenoside.

One of Juliana's earliest stories, *Melchior's Dream*, an uplifting tale about the virtues of family life, is set in a vicarage on Christmas Eve; the vicarage could be Ecclesfield. A few South Yorkshire words are included betraying the author's Ecclesfield origins — for example, Melchior in his dream forgets to 'mend' the fire. Significantly Juliana's surviving commonplace book contains a list of dialect words and their meanings, words such as *smittle* (spread contagiously), *winterhedge* (clothes horse), *loppered* (sour), *addle* (to earn) and *sken* (to squint). Other stories with a local setting or a local inspiration include *The Yew Lane Ghosts* (in which she described Yew Lane in Ecclesfield as 'a loitering place for lovers — dearly-loved play-place of generations of children on sultry summer days'), *The Land of Lost Toys*, *We and the World* and *Our Field*. Her brother Charles sent a copy of *Our Field* to John Ruskin. In a letter to her husband, Juliana told him that she was 'proud to hear he [John Ruskin] says it's not a mere story — it's a poem. Great praise from a great man!'.

One of Juliana's best-known and best-loved stories, set fair and square in the local countryside where the author had spent a great deal of time walking and sketching at the time of its composition, is *Daddy Darwin's Dovecot*, first published in *Aunt Judy's Magazine* in 1881. It is the story of a workhouse orphan (there, was, of course, a workhouse at Grenoside to which the author was a regular visitor before her marriage); about his apprenticeship to an old man who breeds and shows doves; about the theft of the doves and their subsequent retrieval (based on a true local event); about the growing relationship between the old man and the boy; and about the love of the boy for his neighbour's daughter. The setting is the Ecclesfield countryside, peopled by Ecclesfield 'types', speaking the local dialect, and including, as a minor character, the parson's daughter as parish visitor and balancer of the parish charities' accounts.

What better, then, than to leave Juliana Ewing in a corner of a favourite bit of her local countryside, in the final years of her life, surrounded by admirers, as she described it to her husband in a letter in November 1881:

... I have sketched up to-day, but it was cold and sunless, so I did some village visiting. I am known here [Grenoside], bye the bye as 'Miss Gatty as was'! I generally go about with a tribe of children after me, like the Pied Piper of Hamelin! They are now fairly well trained to keeping behind me, and are curiously civil in taking care of my traps, pouring out water for me, and keeping each other in a kind of rough order by rougher adjurations!

— 'Keep out o't leet can't ye?'
— 'Na then! How's shoo to see through thee?'
— 'Shoo's gotten t' Dovecot in yon book, and shoo's got little Liddy Kirk — and thy moother wi' her apron over her heead, and Eliza Flowers sitting upo' t' doorstep wi' her sewing — and shoo's got t' woodyard — and Maester D. [William Dronfield, clog-sole maker] smooking his pipe — and shoo's gotten Jack.'
— 'Nay! Has shoo gotten Jack?'
— ' Shoo 'as. And shoo's gotten ould K. sitting up i' t' shed corner chopping wood, and shoo's bound to draw him and Dronfield's lad criss-cross sawing.'
— ' Aye. Shoo did all Greno Wood last week, they tell me.'
— 'Aye. And shoo's done most o' t' village this week. What's shoo bound to do wi' 'em all?'
— 'Shoo'll piece 'em all together and mak a big picter of t' whole place.'

When the Wild Beast Show Came to Town
The Visits of Wombwells Menagerie

Today we are inundated with images of wildlife from all over the world. On television there are specialist programmes and even specialist channels that take us beneath the oceans, to the poles, into equatorial jungles, and through the hottest and remotest deserts. There we are able to observe at close quarters the domestic lives of animals as varied as the Bengal tiger, the mountain gorilla and the killer whale. Holiday companies take tours to such remote places as the Galapagos Islands, Antarctica and the plains of East Africa. Close-up shots of giant turtles, crowds of Emperor penguins and herds of wildebeest are a possibility for everyone.

In this context it is difficult to imagine that until relatively recently, say forty or fifty years ago, it was only explorers, seafarers and those employed by the government in a military or administrative capacity in the colonies who might have the possibility of seeing wild animals in the flesh and in the wild. No wonder, then, that when a wild beast show came into the vicinity it brought great excitement, and everyone from the highest to the lowest wanted to see the animals. One wild beast show that toured Great Britain, visited not only large cities but also villages, and crossed and re-crossed South Yorkshire, was Wombwells Wild Beast Show or Menagerie.

Wombwells Menagerie was founded in 1805 by George Wombwell, who was born in 1777 in Saffron Walden in Essex. In the first decade of the nineteenth century, Wombwell, who had a love of wild animals and domestic pets, owned a boot and shoe making and repair shop in Soho, and he happened to visit London Docks. A ship which had docked was unloading boa constrictors and he bought a pair for £75. Within three weeks, by showing and handling the animals, he had more than recouped his outlay and decided to found a travelling menagerie. He initially set himself up as a 'wild beast merchant' in Commercial Road, London, and bought, sold and exchanged animals, and started to build wagons to transport them. He employed agents to watch out for ships coming into London Docks with wild animals on board and had them kept so that he could have first refusal of them. He bought the first imported giraffe for £1,000 but it died within three weeks.

At one period there were three separate Wombwell Menageries, but the third lasted only a very short time. The first menagerie was disposed of by George Wombwell's nephew, Alex Fairgrieve, in 1872. After Mrs Wombwell's death in 1862, the No 2 Menagerie was carried on by a niece (Mrs Edmonds) until 1884 when it was bought by the Bostock family, Mrs Bostock being another niece. Mr E H Bostock took over

CATALOGUE OF.
Bostock & Wombwell's
ROYAL MENAGERIE. Established 1805.
1919 EDITION.

Visitors will please compare the numbers with those over the dens, but as additions are continually being made to the Collection, and some one or more of the specimens included in this catalogue may die, it is impossible to guarantee all the numbers as marked, but care shall be taken to avoid all mistakes.

The Lencoryx Antelope.

The Tapir, or River Elephant.

10. Emu, or Australian Ostrich.

The largest of all birds (with one exception, the African ostrich). The emu has neither tongue, wing, nor tail, and every quill on its body bears two distinct feathers. In Australia the emu is coursed in the same manner as the hare is coursed in this country. and it must be a very swift horse or dog that can overtake them.

20. Nosegus, or Slenderbeak Cockatoos, from Australia.

30. Blue and Scarlet Macaws.

40. Blue and Orange Macaws, from the Brazils.

50. Green or Military Macaws.

Macaws are the largest and handsomest of the parrot family. They are principally found in Brazil. Very Rare.

60. The Griffin Vulture, from the Himalayas.

Great discussion has at various times been maintained among naturalists as to whether the well-known faculty of vultures, by which they discover a dying carcase from distances which appear almost in-

Extract from the 1919 catalogue.

as proprietor in 1888, and he was succeeded by J R Bostock Wombwell in 1919, when it was called Bostock & Wombwells Royal No 1 Menagerie.

As a travelling show, the menagerie had to be a self-contained community. It consisted of the animals, their keepers, the menagerie's managers, wagons to transport the animals and menagerie equipment, horses and horsemen and their accoutrements, caravans for the staff, and even a band. Wombwell was reputed to have a stud of 120 horses to transport the show around the country.

As early as 1847, when the menagerie appeared before Queen Victoria, it contained 500 individual specimens including the Syrian gazelle, Peruvian llama, East Indian sacred bull, polar bear, Australian emu, elephants, African and Asiatic lions, panthers, leopards and Bengal tigers. When the animals were exhibited in the quadrangle at Windsor Castle in October 1854, Queen Victoria recorded in her journal that:

> There was a fine collection of lions & lionesses, leopards, a giraffe &c., & a number of very droll monkeys, whom we fed & who chattered away famously. There was also a big & a small elephant, which performed all sorts of tricks … The big elephant afterwards dragged a cart with the Band about, the Band playing the 'Hallelujah Chorus'!! What an idea! …

The 1919 catalogue — which has many illustrations — lists a wide array of beasts including a griffin vulture from the Himalayas, tapir, Indian leopard, jaguar, blue- and red-faced mandrill, armadillo, wallaby, sloth, civet, ocelot, prairie wolf from North America, Canadian timber wolf, dingo, wombat, gnu, man-eating tiger from Madras, Russian bear from Siberia, polar bear brought back from a whaling expedition 'by a Scotch whaler' …. altogether 750 live specimens — with last but not least, Dot, the smallest adult pony living, fifteen years of age and only twenty-six inches (65cm) high.

Each country-wide 'tour' seems to have been planned with almost military precision. Newspaper advertisements gave details of the next town or village to be visited and the itinerary for the next week or month. Visits to a particular place lasted from one day up to a week. The show arrived at a venue from midday onwards and there was a well-advertised grand procession into the town or village accompanied by the band. Not only would the streets of the settlement be lined with spectators, people would have been coming to the roadside all the way along the route. It must have been worth seeing — many of the largest animals simply walked. Others were in as many as fifteen large carriages pulled by up to fifty horses in the nineteenth century. (Traction engines were used later on.) The show was then set up on a suitable piece of land — often the market place. The afternoon was taken up by cleaning out the animal cages, and setting up. Often a visit was hosted by a patron — a local leading light such as the MP, the mayor, a senior military figure and his regiment, or even an archbishop as in the case of York on one occasion. The patron and his guests would have a private viewing in the late afternoon, before the public were allowed in. This was often when the animals were fed. The band played while the middle and upper classes 'promenaded'. Then, during the evening of the first day and in the afternoons and evenings of subsequent days, the general public flocked in. Besides the caged animals, the monkeys and elephants performed, and from the beginning there was a lion tamer who performed with the big cats. At Windsor Castle in 1847 the lion tamer was a

Dot, the smallest adult pony living in 1919.

woman — Miss Chapman — known as the 'Lion Queen'. 'Delmonico' was the trainer of the 'Musical Elephants' in Sheffield in 1878.

The schedule was often tight, especially where small places were being visited. In such places the show would arrive about midday, open in the late afternoon and evening, and then be off again early next morning. The newspaper advertisements show the precision and organisation involved. It must have been like a royal progress, with people going ahead to check on arrangements, and buy food and bedding supplies.

In the East Riding in the summer of 1870, the show visited twelve different places between the 6th and 29th August, starting at Scarborough and going south to Hull before turning inland and finishing at York. Most stops (seven in total) were for one day, with the longest stop being for four days at Hull. The average daily journey between venues was eight miles (13km). The longest pulls were twelve miles (19km) between Bridlington and Great Driffield, and between Hull and South Cave. The only days off were Sundays.

When the show visited South Yorkshire in the autumn of 1878, exhibitions took place over eight days in the cattle market in Sheffield, moving to the smaller industrial settlements of Chapeltown and Hoyland for one day each, before going to the hiring fairs at Barnsley and Rotherham.

Each performance was, of course, great entertainment, especially at feeding times, when the elephants and monkeys performed tricks, and the lion tamer went into the lion's den or the tiger's lair. These were highlights commented on at length in the newspapers of the day, not least at command performances before the royal family, which happened on no less than six occasions in the nineteenth century — 1830, 1834, 1842, 1847, 1854 and 1869.

But the show was also of great educational value. It was seen as bringing the world from the polar ice caps to the equatorial jungles into everyone's experience. The Wombwells and their successors were seen as 'wandering teachers of natural history'. The *Scotsman* on the 10th April 1872 said the menagerie 'did more to familiarise the minds of the masses of our people with the denizens of the forest than all the books of natural history ever printed'. The paper also expressed the view that the menagerie made an important religious point: 'by the greatness and beauty of the creatures proportionately the Maker of them is seen'.

Queen Victoria expressly wanted her children to see the animals. And when the show was at Windsor in 1847, arrangements were made for all 700 children from the charity schools in Windsor and Eton to attend free of charge. When the show moved to Windsor Castle, the queen invited all the boys and staff of Eton College — between 600 and 700 — to attend.

When it came to Chapeltown in South Yorkshire on the 30th October, 1878, High Green School was closed early and this was formally recorded in the school log book. Even when the show was just passing through small villages, it was likely that the schoolchildren would be allowed down to the main road to catch a glimpse of the biggest animals. This was actually recorded in 1877 at a school in the East Riding, its log book for the 23rd October stating: 'Allowed children to go and see the wild beast show pass the end of the village. Think they might possibly gain some knowledge in natural history they previously did not possess.'

WOMBWELLS MENAGERIE
The Great Collection will make a Grand Entry into the Town
THIS DAY (TUESDAY)
BIRTH AT LEICESTER on October 9th of
THREE FINE BABY LIONS.

Sheffield & Rotherham Independent, Tuesday the 22nd October 1878

EDMONDS' (LATE WOMBWELLS)
ROYAL WINDSOR CASTLE MENAGERIE
THE A1 OF THE WORLD
Now exhibiting in the CATTLE MARKET
Open daily at 12.
TUESDAY NEXT positively the LAST DAY in Sheffield
the Collection proceeding on WEDNESDAY to CHAPEL-
TOWN, Thursday HOYLAND, en route, for Barnsley
and Rotherham Statutes.

Performances with the wonderful groups of trained
Animals and MUSICAL ELEPHANTS by DELMONICO
Every Alternate Hour.

Great Additions have been made since last visit to Sheff-
field and the FAMILY OF BABY LIONS only a few days
old now on view.

NB Grand Select MID-DAY FEEDING and PER-
FORMANCE of the TRAINED ANIMALS on MONDAY
at Three o'clock. Admission on this occasion 1s 6d;
children & servants 1s.

Sheffield & Rotherham Independent, Monday the 28nd October 1878

Two newspaper advertisements about the visit of the menagerie to South Yorkshire in 1878.

Visits to Wombwells Menagerie made a lasting impression on a variety of nineteenth-century writers. For example, in Captain Marryat's *Peter Simple* (1834) there is a detailed description of a visit to 'Mr Polito's Menagerie' at Portsdown Fair, generally believed to be based on Wombwells Menagerie. The narrator comments that the menagerie was 'better worth seeing than any thing in the fair'. He describes the tapir, hippopotamuses, the kangaroo, the pelican, the laughing hyena, the royal Bengal tiger, and a large lioness which caused pandemonium by escaping.

One of Wombwells' wild beasts also made a deep impression on the Ecclesfield-born Victorian children's writer Juliana Ewing (see also pages 96-105). In her adventure book for boys *We and the World* (published in 1877), in a section concerned with local moorland bee-keeping, she wrote of a bee that 'the bars of his coat "burned" as "brightly" as those of the tiger in Wombwell's menagerie...'.

The menagerie also mightily impressed Yorkshire's leading nineteenth-century naturalist. Charles Waterton of Walton Hall, Wakefield, was famous for his *Wanderings in South America* (1825). He is also regarded as the father of British taxidermy. He used to spend part of each autumn at Scarborough, and this was a regular port of call of Wombwells Menagerie. On one of these visits, Walton went to the show and saw a female chimpanzee, that he saw was near the end of its life. He arranged to buy it when it died and he mounted it, 'hollow to the very nails', and sitting on a coconut. It has survived to this very day and is in Wakefield Museum.

One very important issue today is animal welfare, and it is unthinkable that a show such as Wombwells would be allowed today. The animals were confined in very small

above   Wombwells wild beast show *en route* to its next appointment.

left   Horse and Tiger public house sign, Thorpe Hesley.

Illustration from the *Illustrated London News* showing Queen Victoria, Prince Albert and the royal children visiting the menagerie in the courtyard at Windsor Castle in 1847.

spaces for weeks or even months, and it was impossible, even if they had considered it, that appropriate conditions could be provided for such diverse creatures as the polar bear and the ostrich. Then there is the question of methods used to make animals perform. I have not found any press coverage condemning Wombwells Menagerie and most commentators — including royal ones — mention the very clean conditions in which the animals were kept. The *Illustrated London News*, as early as 1847, reported on the cleanliness in which the animals were kept, and George Sturt in his auto-biographical *A Small Boy in the Sixties* said that the greatest impression he had of Wombwells Menagerie, when it visited Farnham in Surrey in the 1860s, was not the animals but the strong smell of 'carbolic'. The 1919 catalogue says the 'entire Exhibition is Disinfected Daily with Jeyes Fluid'.

Let us end with a small South Yorkshire historical mystery which may have a Wombwells Menagerie connection. There is a public house in Thorpe Hesley, just a mile (1.5km) from Chapeltown where we know Wombwells put up their show on at least one occasion in the nineteenth century. The pub is called the Horse and Tiger, and is the only one of that name in the whole country. It is believed to have been named after an incident when a tiger in a travelling wild beast show escaped and attacked a horse. The pub sign shows a tiger on the horse's back. An earlier sign showed a wagon on which there was a large cage with the door open and with the escaped tiger attacking a horse pulling a cart. Was the travelling wild beast show Wombwells Wild Beast Show?

Christmas at the Squire's House

A Family Celebration in the early Twentieth Century

In the early 1930s, David Thurstan Smith embarked on a series of articles, published in the now defunct *Blackwoods Magazine*, in which he recalled various aspects of his life in South Yorkshire. These included 'The Bottom Rung', about his two years as a labourer in a Sheffield steelworks; 'A Stockbroker's Memories', about his professional life in Sheffield; and 'El Dorado' a wickedly funny account of an adventure he went on with Earl Fitzwilliam to find pirate treasure on a Pacific island. He also wrote an article full of interest in 1935 where he looked back 'to the days of my youth', about how his family celebrated Christmas. What he described in loving detail was Christmas as experienced by the privileged household of a local squire before the First World War sent the first shock waves through the stability and certainty of a then very hierarchical and deferential world. What is attempted here is to use David Smith's material to give a flavour of a particular gentry family's Christmas in the early years of the twentieth century and to illustrate it with some contemporary photographs.

David Smith was born in 1879, the seventh of nine sons (there were no daughters) of Francis Patrick (always known as Frank) and Margaret Smith of Barnes Hall at Bracken Hill between Ecclesfield and Grenoside. All the boys were educated at Charterhouse. David Smith wrote elsewhere that his parents' marriage was the happy combination of 't' young Squire marrying t' parson's dau'ter'. His father was a landowner (there were estates in Lincolnshire and Scotland as well as in South Yorkshire), solicitor and farmer. His mother was the eldest daughter of Dr Alfred Gatty, vicar of Ecclesfield (see pages 96-105). Mrs Smith died in September 1900, sand it was an exclusively male family whose late Victorian and early Edwardian Christmases David Smith recalled.

The Christmas season began at Barnes Hall on the Thursday in the week before Christmas with a well-attended livestock auction of about forty or fifty beef heifers and eighty or ninety sheep. Butchers came from far and wide, and were greeted before the auction at two o'clock with a meal of boiled beef, apple pie, raisin pudding, and Cheshire cheese, washed down with nut-brown ale. For the next few weeks, house-wives would see notices in local butchers' windows advertising best beef and mutton 'Fed and bred by F. P. Smith of Barnes Hall'.

Once the auction was out of the way, Francis Patrick Smith went into secret conclave with Major, his general estate 'factotum', identifying needy families in the parish. Major was the factotum's name, not his rank. In fact he had been tramping

The nine sons of Francis Patrick and Margaret Scott Smith. Back row, left to right: David Thurstan
Smith, stockbroker. sheep farmer, writer; Godfrey Scott Smith, MA Magdalene College, Oxford,
vicar of Wentworth 1919–27, archdeacon of Furness; Philip Gatty Smith, MA Magdalene College,
Oxford, university boxing blue, country gentleman; Leonard Kirke Smith, Sandhurst-trained
professional soldier, colonel, DSO, served in Boer War, adjutant general of Egyptian army 1920–28.
Middle row, left to right: Stephen Alexander, served as army lieutenant with Imperial Yeomanry in
Boer War, mining engineer, bloodstock breeder; William Mackenzie Smith, eldest son and heir to
Barnes Hall and its estates, soldier rising to rank of colonel, DSO, solicitor (LLD), commander of
local Home Guard 1939–42, president of Law Society 1947, married Lady Mabel Fitzwilliam;
Francis Scott Smith, apprenticed on shop floor at Samuel Fox's (umbrella dept) and rose to become
chairman of the United Steel Corporation; Gilbert Kirke Smith (standing), land agent and factor.
Sitting at the front: George Mackenzie Smith, youngest son, Magdalene College, Oxford (played
billiards for the university), soldier, served in the Boer War and in India, gassed and taken prisoner
at the second Battle of Ypres in the First World War, and he never fully recovered his health.

around the district looking for work when he was taken on at Barnes Hall. He was hired on the condition that he would provide a character reference, and Frank Smith still waited for it fifty-four years later. Major knew everybody's business, and had full details of local people's personal and family problems. He was eventually sent into Sheffield to make necessary purchases.

The 21st December was St Thomas's Day. On that day, popularly called Thomassing, Mumping, Gooding or Corning Day, poor people begged money and provisions for Christmas. Farmers often added a measure of corn to gleaners' pickings from the autumn and winter fields, and this was ground free of charge in some places by the local miller. The tradition at Barnes Hall was that widows visited the kitchen during the day and were given a glass of milk or ale (usually the latter), a piece of plum cake and a sixpence. The last visitors were followed out of the gate by a cart load of coal, a Christmas present for the ladies living in the almshouses on Elliott Lane just outside the grounds of Barnes Hall.

Meanwhile the food for the Christmas festivities was being assembled in the cellars beneath the house. Such were the gargantuan proportions of the Christmas fare that David Smith said it needed 'a generation with leathern insides to deal with it'. There was a beer cellar full of barrels, a port cellar, and another full of burgundy and other wines. In other parts of the undercroft were to be found salted pork from two pigs, a sirloin of beef, a saddle and leg of mutton, pheasants, three or four brace of grouse from the Scottish estate, codfish from Filey, and, of course, the Christmas turkey and the Christmas goose. A large Stilton cheese with a glass of port buried in it was also well in evidence. In a corner were pancheons full of Alderney cow milk waiting for the cream to rise.

Barnes Hall.

In another part of the cellars, neatly arranged on tables, were the presents for the married servants employed on the farm, in the gardens or in the stables: for each family man a sirloin of beef or a leg of mutton, the ingredients for a Christmas pudding, and for his wife a roll of flannel. Single men got a gift of money. These outdoor servants were lined up in the big kitchen on Christmas Eve and, in the presence of all nine sons, the squire thanked each man and presented the gifts.

Then the young men were ushered away to the billiard room while the decks were cleared in the big kitchen for the mummers. The mumming play usually performed in Ecclesfield was the 'peace egg' or St George's play — now called a 'hero-combat play' — and featured a cast of sword-brandishing characters that seems to have little to do with Christmas or any other religious festival. In one version, St George slays the Dragon, St Patrick slays the Prince of Paradine (son of Saladin), the Turkish Knight is slain by St David, a valiant soldier called Slasher is wounded by St Andrew, and the Little Page is wounded by Saladin. The slain and wounded are then all cured by a well-travelled Doctor who carries in his pockets, among other things, crutches for lame ducks and spectacles for blind bumble-bees. The formal performance then ends with Little Devil Doubt threatening the audience that if they do not give money to the mummers then he will 'sweep them all away' (he brandishes a besom). This is the 'bludgy' version that David Smith described.

Having been financially rewarded, the cast was left entertaining the servants under the mistletoe as the family moved to the front of the house, where as the evening passed into night a succession of choirs and carolling groups sang their carols, were given cake and ale and thanked by the squire (no musical fan and known to have said that the only musical instrument worth listening to was the hunting horn).

The final entertainment of Christmas eve was by the Ecclesfield hand-bell ringers. On the floor of the big kitchen they spread their 'deadening rug' and assembled their leather-handled bells in groups. The ringers then knelt in a circle to perform their pieces, and to answer questions about the bells and the bell-ringing technique. As earlier in the evening, as the family made its way back to the billiard room for a final drink before bed, the bell ringers, like the mummers, gave the staff a repeat performance.

On Christmas morning, as the family had their breakfasts and readied themselves for church, parties of children arrived to sing to the housekeeper:

> *I wish you a merry Christmas*
> *A Happy New Year,*
> *A pocket full of money*
> *And a cellar full of beer,*
> *A good fat pig to last you all the year*
> *And please will you give me a Christmas-box.*

Each child was given a new penny, although some 'Olivers' (as David Smith described them) tried for more than one.

Then it was off to Ecclesfield Church for the Christmas service. The family walked it across the fields, but the carriage and horses were got out and the old housekeeper put in it to make sure the footman attended the service. The service was led by the venerable Rev Dr Alfred Gatty, father-in-law of the squire, and then approaching his

Ecclesfield hand-bell ringers, c1913.

ninetieth year. In another article David Smith said that it was Dr Gatty's custom in his old age to have a glass of port and a biscuit in the vestry during the hymn preceding the sermon — 'an excellent thing for a man of his age'.

The exercise of the uphill walk home set everyone up for Christmas dinner. And what a groaning board: a huge turkey stuffed with chestnuts and surrounded by sausages at one end of the table, and a sirloin of beef with roast potatoes, horseradish sauce and Yorkshire pudding at the other; all to be washed down with warmed burgundy and English ale. Then a Christmas pudding mixed on last 'Stir-up Sunday', followed by mince pies, Stilton cheese, and finally nuts and port.

Christmas dinner was a long-drawn out affair with much conversation about field sports, and interrupted and accompanied by Ecclesfield church choir, about thirty strong, who traditionally sang to the family during the meal through the opened dining room windows. The repertoire of the choir included local carols, and David Smith specifically mentioned 'A Song for the Time' attributed to Alfred Scott-Gatty, his uncle, and 'Voices from the Belfry Height' with music by Alfred Scott-Gatty and words by Reginald Gatty (another of David Smith's uncles). Both carols are still sung today in local pubs and other places where the local carolling tradition is as strong as ever.

Christmas dinner was followed by a traditional series of visits to the stables, cowsheds and greenhouses, and sometimes a more strenuous post-prandial exercise such as a game of rugby or other competitive ball games peculiar to the Smiths. They were not allowed to go far because they were all required to provide the audience for further entertainments by singers and performers. These included a performance of another mumming play, the Derby Tup, even 'bludgyer' than the St George perform-ance. And then after supper, what was regarded as the best of the Christmas enter-tainers, the Grenoside sword-dancers, who not only performed their sword dance —

Francis Patrick Smith.

'the finest performance of its kind I have ever seen' wrote David Smith — but also clog-dancing at which they were expert. As on the previous day, they were left in the stone-flagged servants' hall, eating and drinking, and entertaining the servants.

On Boxing Day morning, father, sons and usually also a bachelor uncle ate a breakfast of sausages in their hunting clothes before setting off for the Boxing Day meet at Wentworth Woodhouse. This was what David Smith called a 'foot-people's festival' when locals came from surrounding villages in their hundreds to follow the hounds and track foxes. The horsemen 'did not expect much sport' and it was a general social occasion where

> *Christmas greetings are exchanged with friends staying in the neighbourhood, the best stories hatched in house-parties are whispered around, livers are exercised, shooting parties arranged and we ride home to listen to yet more singers.*

The family's connection with Wentworth Woodhouse was to become much closer than membership of the fox hunt: David Smith's eldest brother, William Mackenzie Smith, married Lady Mabel, the 7th Earl Fitzwilliam's sister; and David's elder brother, Godfrey Scott Smith (the sixth son), was vicar of Wentworth and chaplain to Earl Fitzwilliam from 1919 to 1927.

Grenoside sword-dancers in the big kitchen at Barnes Hall.

The fox hunt at Wentworth Woodhouse.

After the hunt and the departure of the last group of Boxing Day singers from Barnes Hall, the Christmas season came to an end. And gradually, and inevitably, so did the tight-knit family Christmases at Barnes Hall as the sons gradually dispersed to follow their various careers in the army, in the church, in industry and land management. David Smith concluded his article by saying:

All things come to an end, even Christmas festivities. Somewhat weary I take my candle off the beautiful inlaid cabinet and move down the hall to tap the barometer; an old gentleman in a wig seems in the semi-darkness to wink at me from the wall as I make my way to the foot of the stairs, and so to bed.

From Tankersley to Nevada

Population Movements in the Victorian Era

The Victorian period in England and Wales was a period of tremendous population change. When the first census took place in 1801 the population was just under nine million. By 1851 it had doubled to eighteen million and by 1901 it was over thirty-two million. Not only did the population rise rapidly, it became increasingly concentrated in industrial towns and great cities. By 1851, fourteen years after Victoria's accession to the throne, fifty per cent of the population of England and Wales lived in urban areas. By the time of her death in 1901 the figure was almost eighty per cent. This was due to migration from the countryside (out-migration) to urban and industrial areas (in-migration), and high birth-rates among the many young married couples living in urban and industrial areas. The population of the exposed coalfield of South Yorkshire (west of the Magnesian Limestone escarpment running from Thurnscoe in the north to Harthill in the south) rose from 207,000 in 1841 to almost 855,000 in 1911. In Barnsley at the heart of the coalfield with a population of 50,000 in 1911, forty-six per cent of that population had not been born in the town. Similar patterns were also found in the smaller industrial settlements. For example, a recent study by Walker (1993) of mining communities in Darfield parish, immediately to the east of Barnsley, found that in 1881 in four mining communities in the parish with populations ranging from 600 to nearly 1,200, on average migrants (that is people born outside the parish) made up nearly sixty-three per cent of the population. On the concealed coalfield of South Yorkshire, to the east of the Magnesian Limestone escarpment where the first collieries were not sunk until the beginning of the twentieth century, the population of almost every settlement remained stagnant or fell as migrants left to find work elsewhere. Only in Doncaster did the population rise, most dramatically in the early 1850s when 1,000 workmen of the Great Northern Railway and their families were moved sixty miles (100km) from workshops in Boston in south Lincolnshire to the newly built plant and workshops of the company at Hexthorpe.

Internal migration from the rest of the country to South Yorkshire

The vast majority of nineteenth-century migrations were short distance. A team of researchers at Lancaster University (Pooley and Turnbull, 1996), using migration history information supplied by family historians and genealogists on 16,091 individuals born between 1750 and 1930, have shown that long-distance migrations were unusual and that until 1880 the average migration distance was just under twenty-two miles (35km).

This can be illustrated just by looking at the population living on a single road, Station Road in Chapeltown, now part of the A6135 between Sheffield and Barnsley, which was in 1881 one of the most important residential areas lying close to Newton Chambers' Thorncliffe Ironworks and their collieries. At the time of the 1881 census, 686 people lived along Station Road, and 305 (forty-five per cent) of them had been born outside the ancient parish of Ecclesfield in which Chapeltown lay. Of these migrants, 158 (fifty-two per cent) had been born in the rest of South Yorkshire, most of them from neighbouring townships such as Hoyland Nether, Wentworth and Thorpe Hesley, and the nearby towns of Sheffield and Barnsley, although there were also migrants from the rural eastern parts of South Yorkshire such as Tickhill and Fishlake. A further twenty-five per cent of the migrants living on Station Road in 1881 (seventy-seven in number) came from the rest of Yorkshire and the neighbouring counties of Lincolnshire, Nottinghamshire, Derbyshire, Cheshire and Lancashire. The remaining migrants (twenty-three per cent) came from the rest of England, and two each from Wales and Ireland. Most counties of England were represented as birth-places of migrants to Chapeltown in 1881, including a coalminer and a coke burner from Rudham in Norfolk, a railway porter from Over in Cambridgeshire, a labourer from Buckland Newton in Dorset, a housemaid from Newham in Gloucestershire, a druggist's assistant from Southwold in Suffolk, and five people from the tiny village of Babcary in Somerset.

In two South Yorkshire villages there are records of particular concentrations of long-distance migrants in the Victorian period, where in each case 'pioneer' colonists had paved the way. In Hoyland Nether township in 1851, mostly living close together, there were 212 migrants from the Midland counties of Staffordshire (163 migrants),

Station Road, Chapeltown, in the early 1900s.

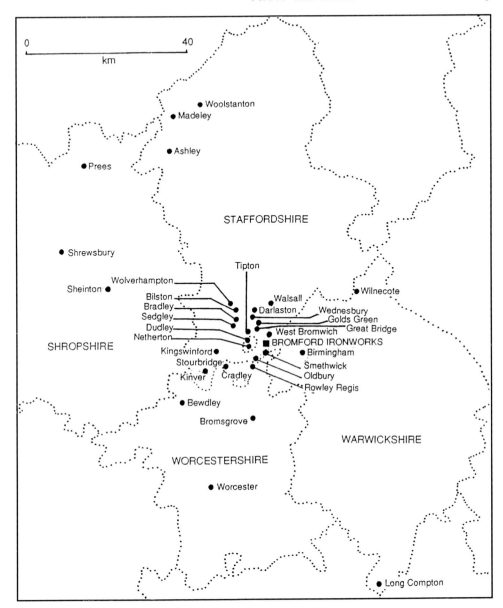

Birthplaces of the 212 residents of Hoyland Nether who had moved from south Staffordshire in early 1850.

Worcestershire (thirty-six), Warwickshire (seven) and Shropshire (six). These migrants had had been recruited and brought to Hoyland by George and William Henry Dawes, the sons of John Dawes, an ironmaster who ran the Bromford Ironworks, West Bromwich, in the 'Black Country' of south Staffordshire. The Dawes brothers had taken on the tenancy of the two ironworks in Hoyland in 1849 and the migrations from south Staffordshire had taken place in 1850. Not surprisingly, seventy-five per cent of these 212 migrants had been born in south Staffordshire, with seventy-one (a third) born in West Bromwich itself where the Bromford Ironworks was situated. The

closeness of most of the birthplaces to West Bromwich emphasises again the importance of short-distance migration: the attraction of employment at Bromford Ironworks had created its own local migration field, like a magnet attracting iron filings.

An even more remarkable example of the long-distance migration of people from a
particular place was to be found in the neighbouring villages of Carlton and Smithies
just to the north of Barnsley, following the flooding in July 1884 of Mostyn Quay
Colliery in the parish of Whitford, Flintshire, beside the Dee Estuary. The *Flintshire
Observer* reported that the 'disastrous occurrence' had thrown out of employment no
less than 200 men and boys. It soon became clear that there was little or no hope of
Mostyn Quay Colliery operating again. Permanent out-migration then began.

Coincidentally, Evan Parry, a native of Mostyn, was made manager of Wharncliffe
Woodmoor ('Old Carlton') Colliery in October 1884. Both his younger sisters
followed their elder brother to the Barnsley area. Anne, her husband Evan Williams
and their four children arrived between 1885 and 1891; Catherine and her husband
David Davies had also arrived by 1890. Both of Evan Parry's younger brothers also
came to South Yorkshire: Enoch and his family seemed to have arrived in the district
by 1888; Evan's other brother David, who was unmarried in 1891, was lodging with
his sister Anne at the time of the census in that year. At the time of the 1891 census
there were also six other families from Mostyn living in Carlton and Smithies,
together with thirteen lodgers of North Welsh origin.

In the 1890s and early 1900s, Evan Parry not only provided employment for a
continued stream of Welsh migrants but he also saw to their physical and cultural
welfare. In 1891 he purchased a partly-built house on Chapel Lane in Carlton
together with two parcels of land on either side of the lane. By 1901 he had converted
the house into three separate dwellings and built twenty-two new houses on the
surrounding land. In June 1902, again under Evan Parry's guidance (he acted as broker
between the landlord, the earl of Wharncliffe, and the Chapel Building Fund Com-
mittee), a corrugated-iron Welsh chapel was opened on Carlton Lane next to land
where Evan Parry had been busy building houses for the previous ten years. By the
outbreak of the First World War, the Anglo-Welsh community formed by immigration
and marriage with local families was between 200 and 400 strong, and Carlton had
become known as 'Little Wales'.

Immigrants and emigrants

Another major feature of Victorian migration was the importance of immigration
and emigration involving millions of people from Great Britain and Ireland. The most
important immigrant group were the Irish, pushed out in their millions by the potato
blight of 1846–7, although emigration from Ireland had been a major feature for a
long time before the great famine of the late 1840s, and was to continue long after. It
has been calculated conservatively that one and half million emigrants left Ireland
between 1815–45 and that three million left between 1845–70. The Irish population
in Great Britain rose from 419,000 in 1841 to 734,000 by 1861. At first the Irish
emigrants were concentrated in London (whose Irish population was 178,000 by 1861
and 419,000 by 1901) and the western ports, particularly Glasgow and Liverpool, but
they quickly spread to other large cities, and industrial towns and villages. In 1861

Evan Parry, born in Gaerwen, Anglesey, 1846, died Carlton, 1912; and his wife Ann (*née* Rogers),
born in Whitford, Flintshire, 1847, died Carlton, 1914.

The Welsh chapel at Carlton (built 1902, demolished 1984).

there were 9,063 Irish-born emigrants living in the exposed coalfield of South Yorkshire — thirteen per cent of the more than 69,000 migrants living there. More than two-thirds lived in the parish of Sheffield, overwhelmingly in the central township of Sheffield, and in Attercliffe and Brightside in the lower Don Valley where employment was available in the rapidly expanding heavy steel industry.

The Irish were, of course, in the majority among the millions of emigrants from Great Britain and Ireland in the nineteenth century who left to seek a new life in another part of the world. And it was the USA that was the major destination. According to government figures (probably underestimates), 2,750,000 people emigrated from Great Britain and Ireland between 1846–55. Of these only 430,000 went to Australia, New Zealand and the Cape Colony. A figure of 2,300,000 travelled to North America, including 1,800,000 to the United States, which had more immigrants from the United Kingdom in those ten years than it had had from all parts of the world in the previous seventy years. In 1853 alone, 937 emigrant ships left Liverpool for North America.

From Pilley to Panaca

One of the best-documented emigrations from South Yorkshire in the early Victorian period to the United Sates was the journey undertaken by members of the Wadsworth family from Pilley in Tankersley parish to Utah and Nevada in the USA. George Wadsworth was born at Pilley in 1827. George was a coal and ironstone miner. He lost his first wife of consumption in 1849 and was left with a ten month old son, James.

Also living in Pilley was George's uncle, James Wadsworth, also an ironstone miner, with his wife Elizabeth and their two foster children Thomas Frost and Mary Jackson. James and Elizabeth Wadsworth agreed to foster the baby James.

James Wadsworth had been converted to the Mormon Church as early as 1841, three years after the first Mormon missionaries arrived in England. In 1846 the Hoyland Common Branch (including Pilley) of the church had twenty members, and this had risen to forty in 1848.

In 1849 James Wadsworth was elected president of the branch and he remained in this position until 1856. In March 1852 he baptised George Wadsworth into the Mormon church and George then became an active member of the church, attending meetings, and engaging in missionary work in the surrounding towns and villages.

As early as 1842 a Sheffield Conference (mission) was formed and in 1849 one of its converts was Elizabeth Broadbent, a cutler's daughter from the Park area of Sheffield. George Wadsworth met Elizabeth on one of his visits to Sheffield and they were married in Sheffield in April 1853. They then lived in Sheffield, where George became a filesmith.

He was ordained a deacon of the Mormon Church in 1854 and a priest in 1855. Later that year George decided to leave Sheffield because of ill-health and he went to live in Dronfield, north Derbyshire, with his brother-in-law William Mullins, resumed working as a collier and became president of the small branch of the Mormon church in Dronfield.

During 1855 the Mormon Church decided to increase the number of European converts emigrating to America by allowing poorer members who could not afford to buy oxen, wagons and supplies for the trek to 'Zion' (the new desert home of the Mormons in Utah) to join. The edict put it this way: 'Let them come on foot, with handcarts or wheel-barrows; let them gird up their loins and walk through, and nothing shall hinder or stay them.'

George Wadsworth, James Wadsworth and William Mullins put their names forward to the European president of the Church, who made a final choice based on years of church membership, age and family circumstances. All three and their families were chosen. George and Elizabeth by then had a baby son Nephi John. James Wadsworth also still had in his family James Wadsworth, George's son, now aged eight.

In May 1856 the two Wadsworth families — nine in all — travelled together to Liverpool, along with their belongings. They had been required to bring, besides clothing and foodstuffs, a straw-filled mattress, bedding, cooking utensils and provision boxes. The provision box had to contain a chamber pot. They sailed on the three-masted *Horizon* on the 25th May 1856. The ship was relatively new and quite large at 1,666 tons. The ship carried only Mormon emigrants: 635 poor and needy, 212 ordinary (who had paid their way) and seven cabin passengers. Everything was well organised with single men and families separated, each with their own berths. A family berth was six feet by six feet (less than four square metres) for four to six people. There were births, deaths and marriages on board, an outbreak of measles and another of dysentery, and much seasickness. One boy was lost overboard. Schools were organised and prayer meetings held. The church elders had supplied thousands of yards of canvas and thread, and after about two weeks at sea the women began to convert the canvas

George Wadsworth, born at Pilley in Tankersley parish in 1827, died at Panaca, Nevada, 1908.

into tents and wagon covers. The captain compared everything favourably to an Irish emigrant ship where fighting and quarrelling were commonplace.

Cape Cod was sighted on the 28th June and the next day the ship was towed to Constitution Wharf in Boston by a steam tug. The journey had taken thirty-six days. Passengers and luggage were unloaded, and the next day they went in cattle cars by rail to Albany (New York State) and then on another train to Iowa City, a journey of more than 1,000 miles (1,600km). Iowa City was the railway terminus at that time. It was by then the 4th July. The rest of the journey for some would be by ox wagon — another 1,300 miles (2,100km) — while for others it would be by handcart.

For reasons that are not clear, James Wadsworth was in the last company that made the journey west to Utah in 1856, but George Wadsworth stayed in Iowa City, and found work and did not travel until the following year. He became branch president of the church in Iowa City.

James Wadsworth's company started the journey west on the 1st August — very late in the season. A wagon train moved at ten miles (16km) a day; a handcart train twenty miles (32km) a day. Across Iowa they passed through settled country, eventually coming to the Missouri River at Council Bluffs. They were ferried across that — both covered wagons and handcarts — and then they were in unsettled country on the Great Plains with mountains and Indians ahead — not something that life in Pilley could prepare them for.

On the 4th October, when the Wadsworths were still on the Great Plains in Nebraska, senior members of the British branch of the church who had crossed the Atlantic on the *Horizon* but who had gone on ahead, arrived in Salt Lake City and reported to the head of the church, Brigham Young. He was taken aback to learn that wagon and handcart trains were still on the way there so late in the season, and he organised rescue teams to go out to meet them with fresh supplies, fresh draught animals, and experienced, fit young men. By the second half of October the Wadsworths were moving into the mountains in Wyoming; fodder for the animals (draught animals and milk cows) was scarce and there was snow on the ground. From then on, deaths were a daily occurrence. At Devil's Gate, a deep gorge cut by the Sweetwater River, the emigrants or 'saints' as they were called, were asked to store all but the most essential supplies so they could travel more lightly. Their possessions would be returned to them the following spring. From that point on, rescuers from Salt Lake City started to arrive. But not soon enough to help James Wadsworth's mother, seventy year old Mary Hutchinson, who died in the mountains. The ground would have been frozen and she would, like many others, be buried in the snow.

Salt Lake City was reached by the handcart company containing James Wadsworth, his wife Elizabeth and their foster son James sometime between the 10th and 15th December, a journey of four and a half months. The following spring, having got all their possessions, they were allocated to the settlement of Payson to begin a new life.

George Wadsworth gave up the presidency of the Iowa City branch of the church in March 1856 and set off with his family in a wagon pulled by two oxen (Brock and Bawly) on the 1st July. Heading west from Iowa City that summer were 1,214 'saints' in 157 wagons and ninety-seven handcarts. As they crossed Nebraska they encountered the same sorts of hazards as their relatives of the year before: frightening thunder and lightning, torrential downpours, stampeding oxen, drownings, and between the 29th and 31st July a herd of 'millions' of buffalo that blocked the trail. Their trek was, however, quicker and much less gruelling than the one the year before, and they reached Salt Lake City at the beginning of October — three months after they set out.

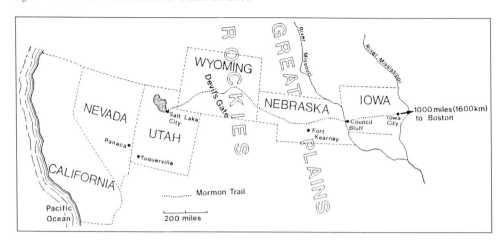

The Wadsworths' journey across the United States.

In 1858 James Wadsworth decided to return to England and take young James with him. George Wadsworth did not like this turn of events — his son wanted to stay — and with the connivance of the Church he 'kidnapped' his own son and the family went to settle in a new settlement called Toquerville, southern Utah, containing five families. They built themselves a dugout 'sodhouse' house built into a bank. They had to survive as subsistence farmers. There were rumours that both the English police and the American government were after them. In 1859 they had a daughter Hannah, another son George William in 1861, Thomas in 1863 and Joshua Charles in 1865.

When the census was taken in 1860 they were so fearful of being found by the authorities that they used the name Allen (George's first wife's maiden name) instead of Wadsworth. The Mullins family from Dronfield joined the Wadsworths in Toquerville in 1860. In 1867 George and his family left Toquerville to make a new life elsewhere. By this time the family felt that detectives were no longer looking for them and the name Wadsworth was used again from 1866.

The Wadsworths moved to Panaca, which is just inside the Nevada border. Panaca had only been in existence since 1865 and was in the form of a timber fort with most of the houses built against the inside of the walls. But soon a town was laid out on the grid-iron pattern. By 1868, 500 people were living there. Panaca's function in the 1860s, 70s and 80s was to act as a service centre for the prospectors and miners in the surrounding area. The Mormons farmed the land and developed freight businesses — taking supplies to the mining towns, hauling timber for fuel and so on.

George Wadsworth with his sons developed a fairly prosperous freight business. George was still an influential member of the Mormon Church and in 1875 became a high priest. The Wadsworths continued to live in Panaca for the rest of their lives and had four more children. George Wadsworth (described in an obituary as 'one of God's noblemen') died in 1908 and Elizabeth in 1911. George William, born in a sodhouse in Toquerville in 1861, was a missionary in Sheffield by 1886 and visited his relatives in Pilley on numerous occasions. Nephi John, who had crossed the Atlantic, the Great Plains and the Rockies when he was less than a year old in 1856, lived until 1932, when he was seventy-six.

Making Ends Meet
Recollections of a Working-Class Village Childhood

As we embark on the twenty-first century we are in danger of taking for granted our current lifestyles and forgetting the unremitting pace of change that was characteristic of the twentieth century. Our great-grandparents, grandparents and even our parents inhabited a world quite different from our own.

At the beginning of the twentieth century, motor vehicles were a rarity, and it was still the age of the horse in areas away from railway stations and urban tram networks. On the farm the horse was not totally replaced by the tractor for another fifty years or more. Heavy manual work in iron and steel works, and coalmines was still the main form of employment for the majority of working men in South Yorkshire and very few married women were employed outside the home. Most children left school at thirteen and many boys went straight into a man's world in factories and collieries.

Families a century ago were much larger than they are now, and housewives and mothers were engaged in an unceasing round of washing, ironing, cooking and cleaning. There was no central heating, no washer dryers, no electric cookers, no electric kettles and toasters, no refrigerators and no microwave ovens. And no pre-packed and pre-cooked meals on the shelves of superstores. The local Co-op was the major source of supplies, and sugar, flour and tea were weighed and bagged in the store. Almost all transactions were in cash. Very few people had a cheque book, and credit cards and direct debit had not been thought of. Telephones were restricted to middle class and professional families. Most people corresponded by letter and postcard (there were three deliveries a day).

Leisure time for children in the early 1900s was spent as it had been for centuries, playing in woods, fields and on the street in spring and summer, and round the fire reading or listening to stories in the winter. In most families, people clustered round a coal fire in winter. The days of a child having his or her own centrally heated room with a television set and personal computer were in the far distant future. The cinema was still an innovation. Church and chapel formed an important part of life with their yearly round of festivals and outings.

Published personal recollections of childhood by people of working-class origins are relatively rare before the beginning of the twentieth century. But things have now changed. With the advent of the tape recorder, the audio-taping of accounts of people's lives — what has become known as oral history — has become widespread, and more and more people have written and published accounts of their early lives.

Arthur Andrews in middle age.

What is presented here are extracts from the recollections of a village childhood. The story is of a boy's childhood in the village of Grenoside, less than five miles (8km) north of Sheffield. The writer is Arthur Andrews who was born in 1900. The poignant and humorous account of his childhood, written when he was in his seventies and eighties, was discovered by his daughter after his death. It is remarkable for a number of things: the detail of the recollections; his working life as a schoolboy; his descriptions of the village workhouse; and the humorous stories he has to tell.

Early home life

I was born in one of the cottages at Wheel Lane Top, Grenoside on 17 January 1900. There were three cottages which stood on the land where the Mormon Church now stands. They were built of stone and were warm and well-kept. I was the fifth living child of Willis and Mary Ann Andrews (née Cooper). We were crushed for room, having only two bedrooms, a living room and kitchen. My father worked at the Silica Brickworks at Oughtibridge. My father's job was to empty the tubs of ganister when they reached him and send them back towards the drift pit. He then shovelled the ganister into the breaker to be crushed to size before being ground to dust. This dust was inhaled by the workmen and resulted in a disease of the lungs called ganister complaint. In my opinion this was the cause of my father's early death.

A surprise visit by Barnum & Bailey's Circus

My father got up for work at 4.45 am and could hardly believe his eyes one morning. The garden was full of animals — donkeys, ponies, llamas and others. He got us all up to see, and there was Barnum & Bailey's Circus. All crowded about the crossroads were wagons and caravans of all descriptions; camels and elephants were eating the hedges and the ivy off the garden walls. The circus attendants were struggling to get the animals from the garden which they had cleared of everything — cabbages, potatoes, all the vegetables in fact.

Grenoside Workhouse

The land now occupied by the former Wortley Rural District Council offices used to be the workhouse gardens and was worked by the permanent inmates of the institution. They wore grey fustian trousers and jackets, and worked hard and kept the ground well planted and tidy. The food produced was used to feed the inmates of the workhouse and the fever hospital above the workhouse. At that time there was a large number of inmates — children of unknown parentage, orphans, aged people and people who were too proud to ask for what was then known as parish relief. This was the only source from which help could come in those days. The men working in the gardens were allowed a copper or two for spending money. Sometimes on Saturday morning they would ask me to go on to Womersley's shop for twopennyworth of tobacco. I would sometimes have five or six lots for which in turn they gave me a penny for fetching it. Sometimes they would slip me a cabbage or cauliflower over the wall, to which the foreman turned a blind eye.

Connected to the workhouse was what was known as the vagrancy ward. This was the part of the buildings that housed the tramps that travelled in those days from one place to another. Our cottage wall to which the chimney was attached faced the footpath. The wall was warm and in winter the tramps would stand against the wall waiting for the bell which was rung at 6 pm. They would then hurry up the lane to the vagrancy ward, there to be named and examined by the workhouse master and his helpers, after which they received a pot of tea, something to eat and a bed.

Barnum & Bailey's circus pays a call.

The group of cottages at the top of Wheel Lane, Grenoside, where Arthur Andrews was born.

Next morning at 6 am the bell would ring again. They were got up, made to wash, given something to eat and drink and then those that were able had to break two barrowfuls of cinders that came from Thorncliffe Ironworks to pieces about the size of an apple. These were used to repair roads before the use of tar macadam.

The fever hospital

Above the workhouse was the Scarlet Fever Hospital, to which all people in Ecclesfield Parish were brought if they contracted scarlet fever or diphtheria. Mr Andrew Wilson was the doctor in charge and he was well respected as was the matron and the nurses. My Aunt Lydia Cooper was the laundry maid there, and a rough job it was. I have seen her hands bleeding from the soda and disinfectants that she had to use on the bedding. On visiting days relatives were only allowed to go up to the ward windows and stand on the steps and converse through the windows. You had to hand any gifts to the matron. The caretaker's name was Mr Wilkinson. If the hospital received notification that there was a patient for the hospital, Mr Wilkinson and a nurse would journey in the horse-driven ambulance to the home of the patient, collect the patient and return to the hospital. If the nurse thought it necessary a man would attend the home of the patient and disinfect it to try to stop the spread of the disease. A patient would stop for a period of up to six weeks or until the infection was controlled. During the latter part of the convalescence they were allowed to mix and walk together in the hospital gardens. We boys would climb up the very high wall and convey messages between the patient and the patient's family.

Main Street, Grenoside. Thackeray Row was a side street off Main Street.

Move to Thackery Row

After our house on Wheel Lane we took a house in Thackery Row off Main Street or Turnpike as we called it. Unfortunately my father died when we had only been there a short time. My youngest sister was born soon after my father's death. That left my mother with the task of bringing up seven children and looking after grandfather. I shall never forget the birth of my youngest sister. I was playing in the street with my sister. Aunt Martha, who was the midwife, was busy with my mother (we learned later). A Tingalary man came up the street with a brown bear on a chain and it was dancing. With yells from both of us, we dashed up the stairs to tell mother, only to be thrown down the stairs again by Aunt Martha!

In the winter of our first year on Thackery Row when hare hunting was prevalent in the villages around Ecclesfield, the beagles, under Tom Barlow, the huntsman, arrived in the village having walked up from the Shrogs. The dogs were put into a stable or shed while the huntsmen went into the pub for a pint. I would have been about five years old and my friend, Willis, and I wanted to look at the dogs. After one or two attempts, between us we managed to get the peg from the hasp that was holding the door. Next moment we saw the dogs alright, we were covered with them, off they went all over the village with the huntsman blowing his horn and all the followers yelling. Willis and I ran to the Angel Inn football ground. If there had been a hare there we should have caught it the speed we went at.

Making ends meet

Money was very tight and finally mother had to apply to the Board of Guardians for help. After consideration they allowed her eight shillings a week. My uncle allowed grandfather five shillings, so that was her full income. Mother used to take the youngest child with her and go out and do a day's washing and earn two shillings two or three times a week. Later my eldest sister went into service at the Pack Horse Inn, High Green for two shillings a week and her keep, and then my eldest brother started work at Oughtibridge Brickworks for tenpence a day. As each one got old enough to leave school the Board reduced mother's allowance by one shilling a week. The third eldest child left school and went into service at Bradfield, she earned two and threepence a week.

Part-time carter and horseman

At the age of nine, I used to walk to Bradfield to collect two shillings of her wage to help the family budget. One day, when I was returning from this errand, going up Stephen Lane, Mrs Ernest Thorpe called me and asked if I would like to work for her weighing coal which she sold by the half and the hundredweight. The wages were to be sixpence a week. I accepted the job but told her that I would not be able to go at dinner time as I had to take dinners to two men at Fox Hill quarry (for twopence a week). She said that was alright, I could go before school in the morning and in the evening and a full day on Saturday.

Sometimes I had to deliver coal to people who could not collect it themselves. I had customers at Wood End, Skew Hill, Topside, and other places and pushing a hundredweight of coal is no mean task. Sometimes the customers would give me twopence for taking the coal, sometimes just grumble. Mr Ernest Thorpe was the carter for Grenoside. He owned six horses and had carts and drays. He carted all manner of things including files and coal. His horseman was a grand chap named John Hobson who was very kind to me. Before long I started to drive a horse and cart and fetch coal from Smithy Wood Pit. John Hobson used to tell me where he had delivered a load of coal so that I could go, along with one of my brothers, to get the coal into the coal place for them. Sometimes he delivered a load of coke to the church and I would go with a barrow and wheel the coke around the church to the boiler house for fourpence. The headmaster, Mr Tom Fulleylove, who was also the church choirmaster, would allow me to go from school at 3.30 pm in the winter to get the coke moved before dark. I would then go to Thorpe's, fill up the barrows or help John to bed the horses down and feed them. Sometimes I would take four horses at a time, riding one and the others on halters, up to St Helena to the fields belonging to Tom May, there they would graze until morning. Then, with a bowl of corn I would coax them to the gate, slip three halters on, climb the gate, and after opening it, mount on to one horse's back and ride down to the stables for about 7 am. John would have tidied round and got their feed in the manger. We would then comb and brush them down; John believed in well-groomed horses. On one occasion, Turpin, a big Shire-crossed horse had a nasty gash on his leg where he had been kicked by another horse when we went to collect him from St Helena fields. The vet came and stitched it and said it must be rested for a while. Later he said we should exercise him by letting him graze on the roadside down by the church. Before I went to school I took him down the road to graze. He enjoyed the grass which at that time before motor cars was sweet and clean and in the summer collected for winter feed. One morning he was quietly grazing when Sam Fairest's motor taxi (I think it was the first car to come to Grenoside) came rattling up. Turpin, being fresh with not working, kicked up his heels and kicked me over the field wall, but he didn't run away and settled after the noise had gone. I climbed painfully back over the wall, got hold of his halter and led him back to the stable. I then went to school saying nothing to anyone. Someone must have seen the incident, for about 9.30 am Mr Thorpe and the headmaster came to our class and called me out of my place. They took me into the cloakroom, gave me an examination and decided I should go home. Mr Thorpe took me home and told my mother I was to stay at home for a day or two. It was not long before I was back on the job.

Winter time was a tough time for carters at Grenoside, no matter where you went it was either up hill or down, and the roads were bad enough without ice and snow. When conditions prevailed Mr Thorpe would still somehow manage to get to Sheffield with his horse and dray, but getting back up to Grenoside was another thing. If he expected difficulties he would leave word with his wife to ask me to meet him, usually about 6 pm at Wadsley Bridge, with an extra horse, to help pull the load up Penistone Road or the Old Road as we called it in those days. I would gear up old Prince, my favourite horse, in the lamp-lit stables, then with a paraffin lamp on the harness and dressed in a thick, warm coat I would get on Prince's back and set off in the dark and the snow to ride to Wadsley Bridge. Grenosiders will remember the story of the Grimsel Steps on Fox Hill opposite the quarries. It was folk lore that a murder had at one time been committed on these steps which were at the roadside and believed by most people to be haunted by the dead girl. I always used to give old Prince a nudge and quickly trot past these steps. When I got to Wadsley Bridge, Mr Thorpe would be waiting and we would hitch Prince in front of Major and get under the tarpaulin dray cover and make our way up the Old Road. There was no necessity to drive, the horses knew their way back to the stables.

The shoesmiths for Grenoside were at the bottom of Blacksmith Lane. Mr French and his sons were the smiths. I used to enjoy taking the horses to be re-shoed (or sharpened in winter time). If he had a horse there already, I would tether my horse and go and work the hand-bellows, blowing the coke fire into extra heat to make the iron pliable for bending into shape. I had one thrilling experience while returning with Major after he had new shoes fitted. He was a youngish horse and had never given me any trouble while riding him. I was going back up Blacksmith Lane, quite comfortably, when a kite that was being flown by a boy in the field ducked down straight in front of the horse's head. He jumped, nearly throwing me off, then set off up the lane at a fast pace. I grabbed hold of his mane with one hand, pulled at the reins with the other, but there was no stopping him. Up Blacksmith Lane, down the Old Road, up Skew Hill and we were nearly at Lane Head before he decided it was enough and settled down. I pulled him up, got off at a field gate, tied him up and sat on the grass until my knees finished knocking. I didn't say anything to John or he might have stopped me riding or laughed at me.

Leisure time

For recreation we had the maypole on May Day and sports and tea parties at Whitsuntide and Christmas. In the winter there were chapel socials, the Band of Hope night being a special night with games and recitations. The superintendent was Bill Senior, an elder of the chapel. The meetings were held in the old Primitive Methodist chapel where the only lighting was a ring of gas jets in the roof. These were lit by a lighted taper on the end of a long pole. This pole served another purpose; old Bill would sit in the pulpit watching the games being played by the children and if he thought you were getting a bit boisterous, down would come the pole on your anatomy somewhere and you settled down. They must have been dedicated people to give their time to give us a bit of pleasure, and teach us religion. There were many good instrumentalists — Walter Sharp, Bill Sharp, Miss Burkinshaw, Lily Sharp, Hector Ellison, Tom Fulleylove, Alice Gledhill, the Nuttalls, Farewell Hobson and his double bass which he and his son, Hugh, carried all over the circuit giving their assistance along with some good voices to other chapels. On one occasion one of the chapels was singing the Messiah and had borrowed a bass player. They were going nicely when the bass player complained that the light was too bad so they asked a boy to stand by the player's music stand with a lighted candle. When it came to the 'Crown Him' chorus the boy

Frenchs' Grenoside smithy.

was a bit fed up and so was the player who was heard to say after each 'Crown Him', 'Howd bloody leet up'.

Christmas time was always a time of music and singing for weeks before Christmas. If you were passing Grenoside Working Men's Club and Institute you would hear melodious sounds of Christmas hymns, some of which were never heard elsewhere. It seemed to be a custom in the old days that each village had its own Christmas carols. As boys we would black our faces, carry a pick, a shovel or riddle and go around the village, including the pubs, singing 'Six Jolly Miners'. Letting Christmas in was also the order of the day for Christmas morning. You would sing the shortened version of a carol, say the shortened version of a rhyme and listen. If you didn't get word you were too early or too late you waited patiently for the door to open and a hand offering you a penny or twopence, if you were lucky. Having a coal round, as I had, proved useful at this time, I would call on all my customers and sing (I had a decent voice in those days) and was rarely denied a copper or two. Nearly every child in Grenoside would go down to visit Mr Bellhouse at Greno House. You had hardly opened your mouth to sing when Norah Cooper, the housekeeper, pushed a penny in your hand — 'Thank you, next please.' No matter how many children went they received their penny, new ones, then old, when the new ones ran out. I have collected as much as 4s 6d and a sore throat carol singing!

Chapeltown Picture Palace in its heyday. The film on show was *'Neath Lion's Paw*.

Chapeltown Picture Palace was built about 1912 and very popular it was, two different shows a week. If you were lucky and had done an errand for Mrs Birch at the sweet shop she would loan you her pass which allowed you to get in for a penny. Of course it meant a walk through Greno Wood , down Barnes Hall park to Chapeltown and back, but who cared! At High Green the only sound was a piano, the pianist tried hard to compete with the picture — horses galloping, cowboys singing, the Charge of the Light Brigade — and pellets of toffee paper being fired from a bit of garter elastic by the boys in the audience. Sometimes the music stopped and Muriel went on strike, and then Mrs Woofenden chased the offenders from the Picture Palace with her stick.

Model Communities or Squalid Living?

Exploring the History of Mining Villages

The coalmining industry not only had an enormous impact on the industrial landscape of South Yorkshire, but also on settlement patterns. Ancient agricultural villages were completely transformed by the influx of miners and completely new settlements were created. Now that mining has almost completely disappeared from South Yorkshire — there are only three collieries still in production compared to fifty only thirty years ago — and regeneration has swept away not only the collieries and their waste tips but also, on the exposed coalfield, some of the settlements themselves, we are in danger of forgetting what interesting histories, ancient as well as more recent, these mining villages have.

The simplest mining settlements were in the form of terraced rows, often next to the pit gates, for example, Long Row at Carlton just outside the pit yard of New Carlton Colliery. The miners' rows at Elsecar (Old Row, Station Row, Reform Row) also come into this category and still survive. At a larger scale are the colliery villages or small colliery towns that grew up in an unplanned way in the

Long Row, Carlton, now demolished.

nineteenth century on the exposed coalfield, either engulfing or built away from existing villages.

Mexborough, Wath and Wombwell are examples of small towns which once housed thousands of miners and their families that developed from engulfed agricultural settlements. Worsbrough Bridge, developed next to a branch of the Dearne and Dove Canal and the South Yorkshire Railway, three-quarters of a mile (1km) south of Worsbrough village, is a good example of a mining village developed away from an existing settlement; and, at a larger scale, so is Parkgate near Rotherham, a combined iron and steel and coalmining settlement, which eventually outgrew neighbouring Rawmarsh.

Perhaps the most distinctive type of colliery settlement that can be recognised in South Yorkshire is the large planned colliery settlement, restricted to the concealed coalfield. This type of colliery village or small town is of twentieth-century origin, the design of which was much influenced by the garden city movement and often contains well-laid-out estates of geometrical design. These settlements were often laid out next to existing agricultural villages and sometimes have 'new' in their names, for example, New Edlington next to Old Edlington, New Rossington next to Rossington, and Bentley New Village next to Bentley. They housed miners at widely spaced collieries, so another characteristic of these planned villages is that they are separated from each other by large tracts of countryside, unlike the colliery settlements of the exposed coalfield which often merge into each other, as in the Dearne Valley between Wombwell and Mexborough.

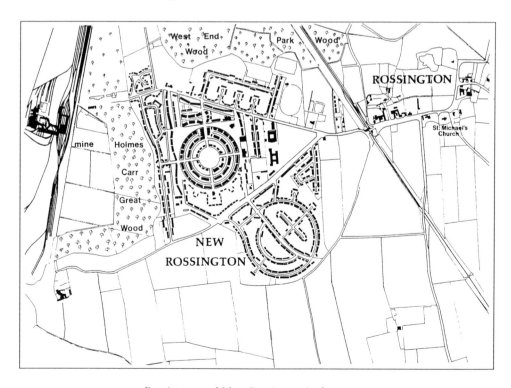

Rossington and New Rossington in the 1930s.

In the rest of this chapter, detailed accounts are given of three former colliery settlements on the exposed coalfield: Dodworth, Treeton and Denaby Main.

Dodworth

A territory called Dodesuurde was named and described in *Domesday Book*, and this had become Dodworth or Dodwurth in most documents by the fourteenth century. The name is Old English (Anglo-Saxon) and means 'Dodd's enclosure'. At some point in the early medieval period, the village had grown out of this Saxon enclosed settlement and assumed a linear shape with the farmhouses of its inhabitants ranged along both sides of a wide street, which eventually became known as Town Street and then High Street.

The site of the settlement was a broad low spur between two eastward-flowing streams. It was dry, and the spur — and the village street — became a section of an important land route that went westwards over the Pennines and eastwards in the direction of Doncaster. It was the salt route from Cheshire and eventually became a turnpike road (Doncaster and Saltersbrook Trust). A house on the southern side of High Street at the western end of the village is still called Salter Croft after the field of that name. Fields with 'salter' names are believed to have been grazing stops for salt-carrying packhorse trains. Two subsidiary settlements also grew up at some unknown date around two small areas of common at Dodworth Green (first recorded in a document in 1557) and Dodworth Bottom (first recorded in 1578).

The main part of the pre-industrial village of Dodworth, on either side of the straight main street between the cross-roads in the west and the Pheasant Inn in the east, has some characteristics of a planned medieval village. The farmhouses of the tenants of the medieval lord seem to have been located on either side of a wide and straight village street, each farmhouse lying at the street end of a long, narrow and straight-sided enclosure called a croft. In Dodworth the crofts stretched north or south until they came to one of the two streams which flowed north and south of the spur on which the village was sited. Centuries of amalgamations, through sale, exchange and marriage, and the building of houses, barns and cottages in the crofts, has complicated the picture, but the basic pattern is still clear.

Research in other parts of Yorkshire has suggested the period from about 1070 to the end of the thirteenth century as the period of origin of many planned villages. There is also a strong correlation in Yorkshire between the existence of villages that appear to have a planned layout and their ownership by high-status lords including the archbishop of York and the heads of monastic institutions. It may be significant that the Norman lord of Dodworth, Robert de Lacy, presented Dodworth to the Cluniac priory of Pontefract in about 1090, and it remained in the priory's possession until the Dissolution of the Monasteries in 1539.

Dodworth underwent considerable change in the nineteenth century as a result of coalmining development. The biggest colliery near the village was Old Silkstone, earlier known as Church Lane Colliery. This had been sunk in 1858 after the coming of the Barnsley branch of the Manchester, Sheffield and Lincolnshire Railway on land acquired by the Charlesworth brothers, the Wakefield colliery owners. The colliery remained in production until 1985.

The development of this colliery and others in the vicinity had a marked impact on population growth in the village. In 1801 the population of Dodworth was only 403. By 1851 it had grown to just under 1,500, the result of coalmining development and domestic linen handloom weaving. This had justified the building of St John's Anglican parish church, where the first service was held in February 1846. There was a sharp rise in population in the 1850s and it had reached 2,117 by 1861. By 1901 it had increased to 3,022.

Unlike in some other places in South Yorkshire, colliery development near the village of Dodworth did not result, in the nineteenth century, in the emergence of a distinct new colliery village separate from or attached to the existing village. Instead there was infilling of gaps within the existing settlement. Some infilling had gone on from the early nineteenth century to accommodate linen weavers and their looms, but by the beginning of the twentieth century these cottages were occupied by miners, and further miners' cottages were built in remaining spaces. Silver Street at Dodworth Bottom, which still survives, and where sixty-one coalminers were living in 1891, is typical of this type of development. The cottages in the in-filled Jermyn

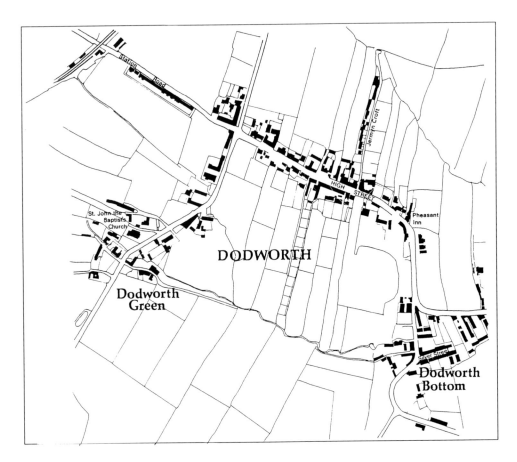

Dodworth at the beginning of the twentieth century, showing its original medieval outlines and infilling of the village with miners' housing.

Croft behind High Street were also the homes of more than forty coalminers in 1891. Outward growth was the exception before the twentieth century, the most obvious example being the thirty houses on Station Road between the Station Hotel and the railway station. The pair nearest the station were built in 1901 and called Belmont View ('belmont' meaning 'beautiful mountain' — in reality, the Old Silkstone spoil heap).

Treeton

In 1819, in his *History of Hallamshire*, Joseph Hunter, the father of South Yorkshire local history, said that Treeton 'stands in a retired and pleasant situation, no turnpike-road passing through it. The inhabitants for the most part are employed in agriculture.' He might also have added that the village was built largely of rose-pink Mexborough ('Rotherham Red') Rock, with thatched roofs adding to its rustic character. It also had a medieval church (a church and priest were mentioned in *Domesday Book*) with a solid stone tower and which contained a fine military effigy dating from the thirteenth century. But this rural face was soon to change for ever. In 1840 Treeton entered the railway age when George Stephenson brought the North Midland Railway through the western part of the township on the edge of the River Rother floodplain. Then, inevitably, came a number of important colliery developments to exploit the rich Barnsley and Silkstone seams that lay beneath Treeton and its neighbouring townships.

The first sod was cut at the sinking of Treeton Colliery on the 13th October 1875. The *Rotherham Advertiser* reported that 'The sun shone brilliantly, and the charming landscape which was soon to be disfigured by colliery headgear and huge chimneys was the subject of much admiration.' The Barnsley seam was reached at a depth of 333 yards (305m) in early 1878, but the bad state of the coal trade and lack of capital caused a closure from September 1878 until the spring of 1882. The population of Treeton grew quickly. It was 383 in 1871, 897 in 1881, and by 1901 had more than doubled to 1,979. Between 1881 and 1903 the company built about 234 cottages in Treeton to house the rapidly growing population of miners and their families. These were in four groups, one at each end of the existing village, one at Bole Hill Row and a fourth further north of this at New Bole Hill. The quarries at Bole Hill provided the stone for more than 100 of these cottages, the rest being built of brick.

It was not just miners and their families who had come to live in the village — men at all levels of colliery supervision and management lived there. The colliery houses on Treeton Wood Lane, for instance, included the 'Big Six', built for more senior men, and there were two specially built detached houses, one for the pit manager and one for the engineer. John Howard Keep, the secretary of Rothervale Collieries Limited, lived at Treeton Hall; and Frederick John Jones, the managing director of the company, lived at Treeton Grange, which he had had built in the early 1890s, away from the village and the pit. (Frederick Jones had a remarkable career with the Rothervale Collieries company. He was appointed manager of Fence, Orgreave and Treeton collieries in 1879 at the tender age of twenty-five. He then became managing director in 1884. He later served two terms (in 1912 and 1913) as president of the Mining Association of Great Britain. He became Sir Frederick Jones in 1919.)

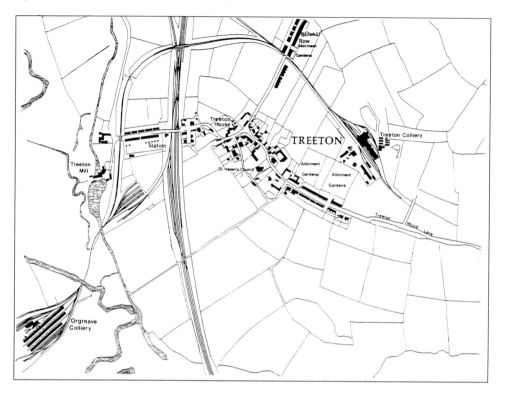

Treeton about 1900.

By the beginning of the twentieth century the landscape was dominated by the mining industry. Besides the enlarged village, there was much development around the pithead at Treeton Colliery, including a coal washery plant built in 1898, a large reservoir, a large and growing waste tip, and a clay pit and its associated brick works. From the colliery a mineral railway ran away north-eastwards, dividing into two beyond Bole Hill Row, with one branch linking the colliery to the Midland Railway network, and the other — the Treeton Colliery Branch Railway, for the most part on a large embankment across meadows liable to flood — with the Great Central Railway network.

The village of Treeton itself saw a number of improvements during the period of intense colliery and related developments in the last twenty years of the nineteenth century. A new board school was opened in 1880 and extended in 1901-2, a reading room was opened in 1888, the parish church was fully restored in 1892, and in the same year a Wesleyan chapel was built. Treeton railway station on the Midland Railway line was opened in 1884. Perhaps the most notable development in the village in this period took place in 1897. In that year Treeton became the first village in England with electric street lighting, installed at a cost of £900. Significantly, Frederick Jones, managing director of Rothervale Collieries, was chairman of the new (1894) parish council, and the electrical power was derived from the colliery company's dynamos.

Treeton Colliery closed in 1990 and, although much of the late nineteenth-century colliers' terrace housing remains, the industrial landscape of the pithead, its waste tip and its railway embankments has been swept away, and the village of Treeton is fast becoming a pleasant suburban village and part of a 'charming landscape' once again.

Denaby Main

Denaby Main, unlike Dodworth and Treeton, was created 'from scratch' in the second half of the nineteenth century on farmland beside the River Don between the villages of Denaby (now called Old Denaby to distinguish it from the mining village) to the the south, Mexborough to the west, and Conisbrough to the east. Sinking began at Denaby Main Colliery in 1864. At that time it was the most easterly coalmine on the South Yorkshire coalfield and was also to become the deepest — the nine foot (2.75m) thick Barnsley Seam was reached at a depth of 448 yards (410m). It was to retain these two distinctions for the next thirty years. Coal production began in late 1867 or early 1868. In 1889 an agreement was reached to exploit the Barnsley Seam under the Magnesian Limestone to the east of the Denaby Main Colliery workings, and in 1890 the sinking of a second colliery, Cadeby Main, began. Production at this colliery began in 1893.

In the forty years following the sinking of Denaby Main Colliery, the colliery proprietors, led by John Buckingham Pope and Richard Pope, West Yorkshire coal-owners, built a completely new pit village to the south of the two collieries. By the beginning of the twentieth century, Denaby Main village provided accommodation for about 2,500 employees at Denaby Main and Cadeby Main collieries.

The structure and shape of the village was relatively simple. To the north of the main railway line lay Denaby Main Colliery, Cadeby Main Colliery and their spoil heaps, and a complex network of mineral railways and sidings. This area also included Kilners Glassworks and some of that company's early housing dating from the 1860s. To the south of the main railway, and predominantly south of Doncaster Road, lay Denaby Main village, containing about 1,500 houses. The housing was in two large blocks, one in Denaby township, the other in Conisbrough parish. Between the two main blocks of residential development lay a wedge of non-residential land containing schools, an Anglican church, a Roman Catholic church, a cricket ground and a football ground. By 1930 this area also contained the Fullerton Hospital, the Miners' Welfare Institute, a cemetery and, at the Doncaster Road end, a park, a market place and a cinema. Doncaster Road contained both housing and a ribbon of commercial development. Lastly, surrounding the village on the west, south and east were extensive allotment gardens.

One of the main characteristic of the completed mining village was the uniformity of it all. Every street was straight and, within each block of development, the streets were laid out in parallel rows of red-brick houses separated in large parts of the village by wide communal yards with blocks of brick-built outside lavatories. Even the pavements were of red brick. This uniformity was carried through in minutest detail: almost all the buildings erected in the fifteen year period from about 1890 — colliers' houses, the villas built for the managerial staff, and the colliery offices — were characterised by a horizontal decorative brick band in the walls and by a triangular tile decoration along the roof ridge. The absence of trees and shrubs in almost all the residential areas emphasised the unrelieved uniformity of the place. The uniformity

Vertical aerial photograph of Denaby Main in 1959. To the north of the River Don are the waste tips of Denaby Main Colliery. South of the river is Doncaster Road running west-east, and to the south of that is the nineteenth-century mining village composed of straight terraced rows all in brick. Allotment gardens surround the village to the west, south-west, south and east.

was even carried through into the street names which, with just a few exceptions, were named after local villages.

It is interesting to record two opposing evaluations of the village within a few years of each other on either side of the year 1900. Mr Eldon Bankes KC, speaking on behalf of Denaby and Cadeby Collieries in 1904, at a hearing held in connection with the 'bag-muck strike' of 1902–3, said:

Surviving villas in Buckingham Road, Denaby Main, originally built for Denaby and Cadeby Main Colliery Company management staff.

At the time when the strike occurred they owned I think some 1,400 houses. They were congregated together close to the Denaby Pit, and they formed the village of Denaby Main. The company had all along taken the greatest pains and succeeded in their efforts in making these houses as sanitary and as comfortable as possible; and, in addition, they had taken great pains to introduce into that village anything that occurred to them to be for the welfare of the men in the way of reading rooms, and recreation rooms and matters of that kind; and I do not think it can be disputed that the village, as owned and managed by this Company was in itself what might be called something equivalent to a model mining village.

In complete contrast, a reporter writing in the *Christian Budget* on the 8th November 1899 under the heading 'THE WORST VILLAGE IN ENGLAND?' said:

I am sitting down to write this article in numb despair, for the mining community I have to describe is so repulsive that many who have never been near it will refuse to credit the story.

The truth lay somewhere between these two extremes. Conditions must indeed have been squalid in the oldest, smallest and most crowded parts of the village. In these areas there were no private gardens or yards, and toilet facilities and water supplies were shared. The proximity of the village to the pits could not be avoided. At least the prevailing south-westerly winds blew smoke and dust away from the village. Some of the housing built for overmen and deputies in Wheatley Street, Tickhill Street and Tickhill Square were very sound and survive today. And in their prime, the villas in Buckingham Road built for members of the colliery management teams would not have been out of place in the most affluent Victorian and Edwardian suburbs anywhere in the country.

Whether the houses of the original colliery village were soundly built or not, or well appointed or not, was secondary to the fact that they were owned by the colliery company. This meant that the loss of accommodation became as much an issue as the loss of wages whenever there was a dispute or whenever a miner was dismissed for whatever reason. There were very few locals among the original 'colonists' in Denaby Main village and no well-developed local traditions and allegiances. And like the working men, the colliery proprietors at Denaby Main were not local, they were determined, experienced, risk-taking entrepreneurs, largely from West Yorkshire. They were determined to make their venture work — and on their terms. These unique circumstances meant that everyone employed by the company tended to fall into one of two camps — they were either union men or company men.

The result of this situation was that every time there was a major dispute between the Miners' Union and the colliery company, the families of the men involved living in company property were made homeless. This happened in 1869, 1877, 1885 and 1902–3. Moreover, as the nineteenth century progressed, the village became larger and larger, and more and more employees at the two collieries were housed in company property. During disputes, large parts of the village had to be evacuated and the population dispersed to be temporarily housed in churches and chapels in the surrounding area, in the houses of family and friends not in company property, and even in tents and in the surrounding countryside, only to return in most cases (and only once, in 1869, in triumph) to the village — but not necessarily to the same house — once the dispute was resolved. The village was therefore not only a convenient place of residence for the mining population, but also a means of social control for the mining company during the years of heaviest investment during the last forty years of the nineteenth century.

In the mid-1960s it was decided that the village, the oldest parts of which were almost 100 years old, was obsolete, and a redevelopment programme was embarked on that would take almost two decades, but which would see Denaby Main rise from the dust as a modern community with the most up-to-date housing and community facilities based on the latest planning principles and ideas of housing design. Ironically by the time the redevelopment of the village was complete, it was no longer a mining village, Denaby Main Colliery having closed in 1968 and Cadeby Main Colliery in 1986.

Relatively little of the physical fabric of the original mining village remains. The entrance to the site of Denaby Main Colliery is marked by a colliery winding wheel and a large part of the surface operational area of Cadeby Main Colliery has been developed as the Earth Centre. Much of the rest of the sites of the two collieries has been landscaped. In the village itself the Roman Catholic church still stands out as an imposing landmark, but the large school built in the 1890s stands empty and the large Wesleyan chapel and the later cinema, although still standing, are used as a bodybuilding and fitness centre and a photographic laboratory respectively. A few streets of houses built in the late 1890s also survive among the modern housing. On Wheatley Street and Tickhill Street there are substantial terrace houses and in Tickhill Square semi-detached houses, their origins betrayed by the tell-tale decorative band of brickwork.

Whit Walks and Going a–Maying
Some Forgotten Calendar Customs

In the past, the year was punctuated in every village and small town by a succession of activities. Although the last century has seen the stubborn survival or re-introduction of old folk customs in Yorkshire associated with the different seasons of the year — amply illustrated in Julia Smith's *Feasts, Fairs and Frolics* (1989) — many more have been completely lost.

Among the re-introductions is Hallowe'en, which is now believed to be of Scottish origin, and which took firm hold in North America and then has re-crossed the Atlantic in its American form, with pumpkin lanterns and children disguised as witches 'tricking or treating' at everybody's front door. Among the stubborn survivals is soul-caking which survives in Stannington, now a north-western suburb of Sheffield. The only other references to this custom of which I am aware occur in Jean Huddlestone's autobiographical *A Geography of Childhood* in which she describes 'Caking Night' in the village of Howbrook between Sheffield and Barnsley. She also mentions it taking place in Stocksbridge. Caking Night (or Cakin' Neet) involved the village children of Howbrook on the 1st November disguising themselves in odd garments, wearing hideous masks and visiting houses, singing on the doorstep until invited inside. The rhyme they sang was:

> My name is Sarah Do
> My age is ninety-two
> I've a hole in my stocking, a hole in my shoe
> Please can you give me a penny or two
> If you haven't a penny a halfpenny will do
> If you haven't a halfpenny a farthing will do
> If you haven't a farthing God bless you.

Jean Huddlestone goes on: 'When we were asked in, we stood mute lest our voices betrayed us. If we could not be identified we earned sixpence.' If they were identified they were given a piece of cake, usually parkin. The tradition in Stannington is now usually an adult one with costume parades and unmasking ceremonies in local pubs.

But such survivals are very much the exception and probably a dozen others have completely or virtually disappeared. These include Plough Monday, Collop Monday, May Day celebrations, Whitsuntide visiting, Whit walks and sings, hospital parades and St Thomas's Day.

Plough Monday was the first Monday after the twelfth day of Christmas (6th January) and was the day that farmworkers went back to work after the Christmas break to start ploughing the fields in readiness for the spring sowing. The custom was that the common plough, which was kept in the parish church for the use of anyone in the community who did not have their own plough, was blessed by the parish priest, decorated and paraded around the village by ploughboys ('plough bullocks' or 'stots'). Money collected from householders was used to maintain the 'plough lights' (candles) which were kept burning in the church to ensure divine blessing on the spring ploughing.

The first reference to parading a plough around a village dates from 1413. The rights to have the plough blessed and plough lights lit in church were abolished at the Reformation, but in the succeeding centuries the blessing of the plough was re-instated in some churches (as it still is in Exeter, Salisbury and Goathland in North Yorkshire) and the plough parade was revived by young farmworkers who collected money for themselves for alcoholic drink, which was often accompanied by plough plays (one of which still survives at Revesby in Lincolnshire), singing and reciting.

The custom of the plough parade had virtually disappeared in South Yorkshire by the First World War. Fred Kitchen in his *Brother to the Ox* (1940) vividly describes the revival of the custom in the Maltby area in 1905. He prefaces his description by saying that the custom even then was 'more honoured in the breach than the observance and was, even at that time, dying out'. He then describes the young ploughmen dragging the plough around the village, singing at all the big houses and 'such as were likely to give them ale money'. This was highly successful, for the plough had to be left in the yard at the Black Swan for several days as none of the party was capable of taking it away for several nights. They sang a song at every place where they stopped, each verse ending with:

> We've ploughed a fair acre, I swear and I vow,
> We're all jolly fellows that follow the plough!

The only later reference to Plough Monday being enacted is in the hospital parade at Ecclesfield in the 1930s, when plough bullocks with blacked faces and dressed in farmworkers' smocks, wearing top hats and carrying pigs' inflated bladders, pulled a plough along the collecting route. They made particularly long stops at local hostelries.

Collop Monday was part of Shrovetide which also included Egg Saturday, Quin-quagesima Sunday and Shrove Tuesday (Pancake Day). Collop Monday was a day of games and dancing, and feasts to consume the food that was forbidden during Lent. This became an occasion for better-off people to supplement the meat diet of their poorer neighbours. Sidney Oldall Addy in the supplement to his *Sheffield Glossary* (1891) links the Collop Monday and Shrove Tuesday customs in South Yorkshire in these words: 'On this day poor people go to their richer neighbours to beg a *collop* or slice of bacon, to supply the fat in which pancakes are baked on the following day.'

In some parts of the country, Collop Monday evening was called Lent-shard Night, when children went round their village chanting verses and hoping to be given food or money towards the Shrove Tuesday festivities. Those doors that evoked no response to their chanting and knocking were pelted with pieces of broken crockery. Scholars

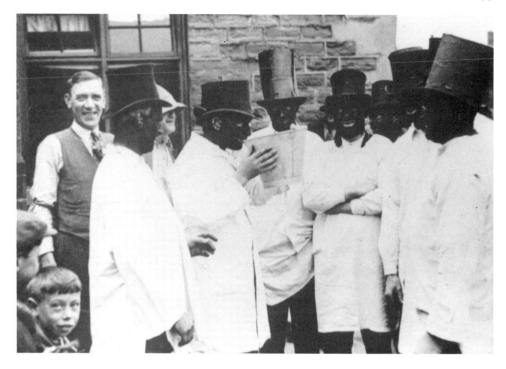

The plough bullocks stopping for refreshment at the Ball Inn, Ecclesfield, during the Ecclesfield Hospital Parade in the 1930s.

at Eton College used to compose valedictory verses to be recited on Collop Monday as a farewell to the rich food and wine that they would not be allowed to consume again until the end of the Lenten fast. Collop Monday, now a completely forgotten custom, became formalised on earl Fitzwilliam's South Yorkshire estate in the nineteenth century, where it was one of two very important calendar customs that involved all employees outside the mansion, as we shall see below.

There were several customs traditionally associated with May Day: gathering the may (hawthorn blossom), bathing in May dew, decorating houses with greenery, making wreathes and garlands, the installation of a May queen (and sometimes a May king) and, of course, dancing round the maypole. And these have now virtually disappeared from South Yorkshire.

'Going a-maying' in the countryside to bring in greenery and spring flowers was recorded as early as 1240 when Bishop Grosseteste of Lincoln complained about priests taking part in 'games which they call bringing-in of May'. From the mid-sixteenth century, voices of disapproval were raised against the practice from reforming Protestants, mainly on moral grounds: they complained about young people going out into the woods on May Day eve and staying out all night — one complainant said that he had heard that of every 'three score, or a hundred maides going to the wood over night, there have scarcely the thirde parte of them returned home againe undefiled'. Going a-maying was banned during the Commonwealth years but returned after the restoration of Charles II and survived until the nineteenth century. Juliana Horatia Ewing, the Ecclesfield-born children's writer (see pages 96-105), in an article in her mother's *Aunt Judy's Magazine* in 1874 encouraging the continuation of May Day traditions, concluded by saying that 'To go a-Maying "to fetch the flowrès fresh" is indeed the best part of the whole affair'.

While returning at dawn to the village on May morning, it was thought bathing in May dew was beneficial to the complexion, could cure sore throats and would strengthen weakly children. Particularly healthful was the dew from oak trees and hawthorn bushes. Samuel Pepys, the diarist, recorded his wife going to 'a little ayre' [retreat] at Woolwich on the 28th May 1667 'and to lie there tonight and so to gather May dew tomorrow morning … to wash her face with'. Again, sadly, this tradition is long gone.

In the nineteenth and twentieth centuries, May Day in South Yorkshire, as in most of the rest of the country, became essentially a children's festival, having been taken over by Sunday schools and day schools. This involved the making and parading of May garlands, the election of a May queen and sometimes a May king, together with footmen and maids of honour and, of course, dancing round a maypole — the possible origin of the maypole as a phallic symbol being conveniently or genuinely forgotten.

Another once-important calendar custom which has virtually disappeared is the Whit walks, Whit sings, and 'big house' and 'new clothes' visiting, which all seem to be nineteenth-century inventions replacing the medieval church wakes and feasts. But they have all but disappeared in the last twenty-five years, after Whit Monday was

Maypole dancing in the village of Howbrook between Sheffield and Barnsley in the late 1920s.

Whit sing at the Ten Acre, Mortomley, in 1930, with Thorncliffe Ironworks in the background.

replaced as a Bank Holiday by Spring Bank Holiday. The Whit Monday walk and sing was seen by many as the most important communal event of the year, with crowds of many hundreds and in some cases thousands taking part, with the children wearing their new Whit suits and frocks.

Stanley Ellam in his book *High Green in the 1920s* recalled the Whit walks and sing in the High Green and Chapeltown area. On Whit Monday morning, the various Sunday schools from the chapels at Stoneygate, Potter Hill, Wortley Road and St Saviour's Church gathered together first on Mortomley Hill and then on the Ten Acre. (This was a piece of ground opposite Thorncliffe Lane owned by Newton Chambers and consisted mainly of pit hills.) The scholars, teachers and parents of the Chapeltown chapels of Mount Pleasant, Warren, Station Road, Burncross and Greenhead, and St John's Church went to Chapeltown market place and sang there, before walking, with their chapel banners flying, to the Ten Acre where a combined sing was held with the High Green contingent. In the afternoon the scholars from the ten Sunday schools went to their respective establishments for a tea and sports.

Sunday school scholars and their teachers also used to visit the big houses of the district and sang on the lawns before the house and received refreshments. For example, Burncross Chapel went to Barnes Hall until well in the 1950s; the Wesleyan and Primitive Methodist chapels from Grenoside went to Whitley Hall again until the

the 1950s; and Birley Carr Chapel scholars near Wadsley Bridge were singing in the grounds of Birley House from the 1870s.

Lastly, it was the custom in South Yorkshire for children to visit neighbours' houses wearing their new Whitsuntide clothes and to receive a small amount of money in return. As a young schoolteacher in Sheffield in the 1960s I remember receiving absence notes from children's parents stating that their son or daughter had been absent from school for a morning, afternoon or a whole day because they had been taken shopping for their new Whitsuntide clothes — usually to the Co-op.

All the customs discussed so far have their origins in the medieval period at least. But even some customs introduced relatively recently have come and gone. In the days before the National Health Service was introduced, hospitals depended for a substantial amount of their money on bequests, endowments and public generosity. Much money was raised throughout South Yorkshire through hospital parades. The villagers of Ecclesfield, for example, mounted a hospital parade from the 1890s until the late 1930s. It was not revived after the Second World War. The custom involved constructing and decorating colourful floats, parading them around the district and, with the help of collectors in fancy dress, collecting donations for the local hospitals.

In Ecclesfield, floats were made by a number of families living in a particular group or row of houses in different parts of the district. Everything was done in secrecy because the floats were part of a competition, with the winner leading the whole parade. Once the theme for the float was decided upon, an expert metalworker or woodworker from within the group of families would make the frame, which was then cleverly covered with coloured paper and other materials.

Themes for floats varied enormously, from local buildings such as Ecclesfield Church, local industries such as quarrying, to more exotic subjects such as windmills

Ecclesfield Hospital Parade assembling on Ecclesfield Common in June 1909.

A group of Ecclesfield Hospital Parade collectors in 1906, all in disguise and in fancy dress, and with highly decorated bicycles.

and royal coaches. Figures of wild animals also featured regularly, such as elephants and a large swan with its cygnets (children in fancy dress) on its back. As time went on, more modern subjects made their appearance such as aeroplanes and cameras. The floats had to be ready for the Saturday afternoon of the third weekend after Whitsun-tide, when they were taken to Station Road pulled by horses decked out in smart leather straps, shining brasses and brightly coloured ribbons.

The collectors who accompanied the parade on foot or on bikes were as colourful as the floats and the people on them. A favourite outfit for the collectors was that of a clown; some went as gypsy girls; others had blacked faces or wore masks.

Once assembled, the parade set off along Ecclesfield Common, up Church Street to Grenoside, down to Wadsley Bridge and past the Sheffield Royal Infirmary to the bottom of the Moor. From there the return journey went through central Sheffield, up the Moor and High Street to the Wicker, then up to Firth Park, on Bellhouse Road to Shiregreen, and down Barnsley Road back to Stocks Hill in Ecclesfield. By then it would be eight o'clock at night, and those with the energy went to the feast beside the Ball Inn.

On Sunday afternoon, there was a sing in Bank House gardens in Ecclesfield, and then on Monday evening the parade re-assembled. It proceeded up the hill to Chapeltown, up Burncross and along to the Crown Inn, turned off to the Rose Inn, down through High Green and Lane End, turned on to Sussex Road and then Station Road, and usually ended up at Chapeltown Feast.

The only place where communal activities related to collecting for local hospitals is known to have persisted into recent times is at Mapplewell, where the Mapplewell and Staincross Hospital and Comforts Fund celebrated the centenary of their hospital sing in 1986, the event having taken place every year since the first such sing on the 31st July 1887.

Towards the end of the calendar year came St Thomas's Day on the 21st December, the winter solstice, and the shortest day and longest night of the year. On that day, poor people begged money and provisions for Christmas (see also page 117). Although long forgotten now, in the nineteenth century the St Thomas's Day custom had become formalised and institutionalised on earl Fitzwilliam's home estate in South Yorkshire. Regular employees were given a quantity of beef and a sum of money (sixpence in the 1840s) on St Thomas's Day. It is not clear when the custom in its nineteenth-century form originated, or when it ceased to operate, but detailed records have survived in the Wentworth Woodhouse Muniments in Sheffield Archives for the periods 1811–28 and 1841–56, in the time of the fourth earl (succeeded to the Wentworth estates in 1782 and died in 1833) and the fifth earl (succeeded in 1833 and died in 1857).

The Fitzwilliam home estate in South Yorkshire was centred on Wentworth Park with its great Palladian mansion of Wentworth Woodhouse (see pages 71-4). It was not only a large country estate in the nineteenth century; it also contained important industrial communities centred around ironworks, collieries and ironstone pits.

The fourth and fifth earls Fitzwilliam were exceptional employers and are described by Graham Mee in his book *Aristocratic Enterprise* as 'archetype[s] of the paternalist for whom the poor were indeed children to be cared for and controlled in a fatherly manner'. This paternalist approach to their employees extended to making sure that there was a safe working environment in the coal and ironstone pits, prohibiting the use of female labour in their collieries which was a widespread practice locally, providing housing of a superior kind for many of their employees, providing free medical care, and providing pensions (including widows' pensions) and accommodation in almshouses for the old and needy. The institutionalisation of the St Thomas's Day tradition was an extension of this paternalist approach.

It was to the employees in the countryside and in the industrial enterprises on the estate that the charity was extended. The 'rule of admissibility' to the charity was: 'Any person regularly employed in the Service of Earl Fitzwilliam and employed at that time. Persons employed at that time at a merely occasional job are not entitled.' Servants at the mansion were not included.

The operation of the charity was a massive undertaking. In 1841, for example, there were just over 1,000 recipients. The largest group consisted of miners, 181 at Elsecar New and Jump Colliery, 168 at Elsecar Old Colliery, 126 at Parkgate Colliery, 55 at Strafford Main Colliery, 54 at Stubbin Colliery, 24 at the ironstone grounds in Tankersley Park and 12 constructing the Thorncliffe Drift, a major mine drainage project stretching from Elsecar to Thorncliffe. There were also 54 persons employed at Elsecar Ironworks and 65 employed on building 'Greasbro New Coach Road'.

Another large group of employees included in the list were those engaged on expanding or maintaining the fabric of the estate, and these included 40 carpenters, 35 masons, 8 sawyers, 6 joiners and 4 plumbers. The agricultural land and estate woodlands provided 61 farm labourers at the home farm, 19 woodmen and 5 blacksmiths. The pleasure grounds at Wentworth, and the parks at Wentworth and

Queuing for the St Thomas's Day charity at Wentworth Woodhouse.

Tankersley, provided 36 gardeners, 7 botanical gardeners, 9 gatekeepers, 6 employed at the menagerie, 3 gamekeepers, 3 park keepers, 8 at the stud, 2 saddlers, a 'boat tenter' at the lakes, a rat catcher and a 'stable bed maker'. The list also included 3 tailors, 3 maltsters, 2 millers, a brewer and brewer's assistant, 2 painters, a cooper, a butcher and a postman. Additionally, 12 former employees were listed who were resident at the hospital (almshouses).

There was clearly scope for mistakes to be made: people being omitted; people claiming the charity who were not eligible; people being given their meat and money more than once. To avoid mistakes, lists were drawn up, but things still did not always go smoothly, and at the back of the 1841 lists there is a set of 'Memoranda for Guidance for another year'. These notes stipulated that, in future, heads of department had to draw up lists of 'admissible persons' and to deliver these to the estate office on the 18th December for the St Thomas's Day 'donation' on the 21st December. 'Serving' began at ten o'clock in the morning.

Every recipient had to turn up in person and each head of department had to 'attend at the time of delivery to identify his men'. Anyone who did not turn up did not receive the charity, and anyone who turned up but was not listed had to wait till the end to see if there was any meat left over. The St. Thomas's Day list was then used as the basis of the Collop Monday charity three months later, when the same employees where given beef and bacon. The surviving lists contain the ticks, question marks and crosses inserted as the serving progressed. There is also a detailed note for 'the person who superintends the cutting of the beef'. This was another enormous task for St Thomas's Day in 1841 involving the butchering of five bulls.

Bibliography & Further Reading

Were Your Ancestors Vikings?

Cameron, K. *English Place Names* (Batsford, new edition, 1996), Ch 6, 'Scandinavian Place-names'.

Crawford, B E (ed). *Scandinavian Settlement in Northern Britain* (Leicester University Press, 1995).

Jones, G. *A History of the Vikings* (Oxford University Press, 1984; republished under the title *The Vikings* by the Folio Society, 1997).

Kellett, A. *The Yorkshire Dictionary of Dialect, Tradition and Folklore* (Smith Settle, new edition 2002).

Richards, J. *Blood of the Vikings* (Hodder & Stoughton, 2001).

Rogers, K H. *Vikings and Surnames* (William Sessions Ltd, 1991).

Smith, A H. *The Place-names of the West Riding of Yorkshire*, Part I (Cambridge University Press, 1961).

Ivanhoe, Robin Hood and all That

Holt, J C. *Robin Hood* (revised and enlarged edition, Thames and Hudson, 1989).

Simpson, J, and Roud, S. *A Dictionary of English Folklore* (Oxford University Press, 2000).

Yates, H. '"Ivanhoe" Illustrated' in John Guest, *Historic Notices of Rotherham* (Robert White, 1879).

'Buildid of Wood'

Beswick, P. *Bishops House* (Sheffield City Museums information sheet 16, 1981).

Innocent, C F. *The Development of English Building Construction* (Cambridge University Press, 1916).

Jones, M. 'Kirkstead Abbey Grange: Part 1 — speculations on its origins', in *Ivanhoe Review* no 4, spring 1993.

Ryder, P. *Timber-framed Buildings in South Yorkshire* (South Yorkshire County Council, 1979).

'The Plucking Down of Religious Houses'

Aveling, J W. *The History of Roche Abbey* (1870).

Beastall, T W. 'An Abbot in Retirement', in *Aspects of Doncaster: Discovering Local History*, ed Brian Elliott (Wharncliffe Publishing, 1997).

Cross, C, and Vickers, N. *Monks, Friars and Nuns in Sixteenth Century Yorkshire* (Yorkshire Archaeological Society, 1995).

Jennings, B. *Yorkshire Monasteries: Cloister, Land & People* (Smith Settle, 1999).

Knowles, D. *Bare Ruined Choirs* (Cambridge University Press, 1976).

'Halfway to the North Pole'

Bostwick, D. *Sheffield in Tudor and Stuart Times* (Sheffield City Museums, 1985).

Hey, David. *A History of Sheffield* (Carnegie Publishing, 1998).

Jones, M. 'The Custody of the Scotch Queen', in *Yorkshire Journal* 27, autumn 1999.

Postles, D. *Sheffield in 1581* (Sheffield City Libraries, 1981).

Ronksley, J G. *An exact and perfect survey and view of the Manor of Sheffield with other lands by John Harrison, 1637* (Robert White & Co, 1908).

Scurfield, G. 'Seventeenth-Century Sheffield and its Environs', in *Yorkshire Archaeological Journal* vol 58, 1986.

Wigfull, J R. 'The Court Leet of the Manor of Sheffield, April 1578', in *Transactions of the Hunter Archaeological Society* vol 3, 1929.

Two Planned Medieval Towns
Beastall, T W. *Portrait of an English Parish church: St Mary's Parish Church, Tickhill* (nd).
Beastall, T W. *Tickhill — Portrait of an English Country Town* (Waterdale Press, 1995).
Holland, D. 'Bawtry — History in the Townscape', in Brian Elliott (ed), *Aspects of Doncaster: Discovering Local History 2* (Wharncliffe Publishing, 1999).

Stone Dragons and Wooden Knights
Bottomley, F. *Yorkshire Churches* (Alan Sutton, 1993).
Jenkins, S. *England's Thousand Best Churches* (Allen Lane, 1999).
Jones, M. 'The Church in the Landscape', in *The Making of the South Yorkshire Landscape* (Wharncliffe Publishing, 2000).
Pevsner, N. *The Buildings of England, Yorkshire: The West Riding* (Pelican Books, 1959).
Ryder, P. *Saxon Churches in South Yorkshire* (South Yorkshire County Council, 1982).

A Unique Historic Rural Landscape
Doncaster Council's Recreational and Cultural Services Department has produced an attractive and useful Fishlake Heritage Trail leaflet. It includes a five and a half mile (9km) heritage trail along the river, and along country and green lanes.

'Leasing, Building and Baptising'
The details of Thomas Watson-Wentworth's visit to Ireland in 1713 are recorded in Abraham Nickson's Irish general accounts 1707–13 and his timber accounts 1713–19, respectively A758 and A760 in the Wentworth Woodhouse Muniments in Sheffield Archives. The first marquis of Rockingham's rent roll book is item A1273 in the Wentworth Woodhouse Muniments in Sheffield Archives.

'Christians are Handier than Horses'
Royal Commission on Children's Employment (Mines), 1st Report (1842) Parts I and II, Parliamentary Papers (380) XV and (381) XVI, Irish University Press.

From Tankersley to Nevada
Coleman, T. *Passage to America* (Hutchinson, 1972).
Free Vanderbreek, H. *George Allen Wadsworth — Pilley to Panaca* (Gateway Press, 1983).
R F Foster. 'Ireland Abroad', chapter 15 in *Modern Ireland* (Penguin books, 1989).
Jones, M. 'A sponsored migration from Staffordshire to Hoyland in the mid-nineteenth century', in B Elliott (ed), *Aspects of Barnsley, Discovering Local History 5* (Wharncliffe Publishing, 1998).
Jones, M. 'Long-distance migrants and cultural identity: the example of a Welsh colony in South Yorkshire', *The Local Historian*, 26, no 4, November 1996.
Jones, M. 'Little Wales in South Yorkshire', *Yorkshire Journal* 26, summer 1999.
Pooley, C G, and Turnbull, J. 'Migration and mobility in Britain from the eighteenth to the twentieth century', *Local Population Studies*, no 57, autumn 1996.
Walker, A G. 'Migration into a South Yorkshire Colliery District, 1861–1881', *Northern History* vol XXIX, 1993.

Model Communities or Squalid Living?

Coates, B E, and Lewis, G M. *The Doncaster Area* (British Landscapes through Maps series, Geographical Association, 1966).

Alan Godfrey edition. Old Ordnance Survey Maps: Dearne Valley & Barnsley, (1908–13); Dodworth (1904); Treeton & Orgreave Colliery (1901).

Jones, M. 'Denaby Main: the development of a South Yorkshire mining village' in B Elliott (ed), *Aspects of Doncaster: Discovering Local History, Volume 2* (Wharncliffe Publishing 1999).

Marshall, J D. 'Industrial Colonies and the Local Historian', *The Local Historian*, vol 23, no 3 (1993).

Whit Walks and Going a-Maying

Baker, M. *Folklore and Customs of Rural England* (David & Charles, 1974).

Ellam, S. *High Green in the 1920s* (Chapeltown & High Green Archive, 1994).

Ewing, J H. 'May-Day, Old Style and New Style' (*Aunt Judy's Magazine*, 1874).

Huddlestone, J. *A Geography of Childhood* (Chapeltown & High Green Archive, 1995).

Kitchen, F. *Brother to the Ox* (Penguin Books Ltd, 1983).

Simpson, J, and Roud, S. *A Dictionary of English Folklore* (Oxford University Press, 2000).

Smith, J. *Fairs, Feasts and Frolics: Customs and Traditions in Yorkshire* (Smith Settle, 1989).

Index